Longaker, Richard P
    The Presidency and individual liberties.   Ithaca, N. Y.,
Cornell University Press ₍1961₎

    239 p.   23 cm.   (Cornell studies in civil liberty)

    1. Presidents—U. S. 2. Executive power—U. S. 3. Civil rights—
U. S.   ɪ. Title.

JK518.L6   353.03   61–8206 ‡

CORNELL STUDIES IN CIVIL LIBERTY

The Presidency and Individual Liberties

The Presidency and Individual Liberties

By RICHARD P. LONGAKER

Cornell University Press

ITHACA, NEW YORK

TO

Emily D. Longaker

Edwin P. Longaker

Preface

THE American presidency is not unique among political institutions in having responsibility thrust upon it against its will. Events and public expectations in this century have transformed the office into the nerve center of national effort in many fields, including international leadership in the Cold War and the guardianship over national prosperity. This study deals with a third major addition to presidential responsibility in the twentieth century—the constitutional obligation of the chief executive to protect individual liberty. The Supreme Court and Congress have received their share of commentary in this regard. The commentary on the presidency, however, is fragmentary and unrelated to any broad recognition of a firmly based presidential obligation. It is the purpose of this book to delineate the nature of this obligation, to describe the available instruments for presidential action, and to suggest the price of presidential indifference.

An attempt to bind together two of the most complex elements of American constitutionalism, the presidency and constitutional liberty, calls for the imposition of certain restrictions which are at once artificial and necessary. First, it is understood that executive action or inaction can affect liberty in a multitude of ways: by its success in maintaining national security in the face of domestic and international threats, by presidential opposition to concentrations of power in our industrialized society, or by encouraging a sound educational environment and a thriving system of private property. All, and others, are necessary if constitutionalism is to survive. What is described here is only one part of the total effort—that is, the specific application of presidential power as a means for protecting and extending traditional individual liberties, the civil liberties of due process of law, the First Amendment freedoms, and the civil rights of minorities.

Second, the writer is fully aware of the pitfalls which are encountered when the terms presidency and executive branch are used interchangeably. There may be a great distance and disagreement in policy and attitudes between the two, as well as a disparity in the configuration of political power. When this disparity is significant, it will be recognized as such; but because the ultimate constitutional authority over the executive branch inheres in the President, it will be assumed that when his subordinates act they do so in his name and when he commands they should obey. The President is constitutionally responsible for the actions of these subordinates. Doubtless President Truman had this partly in mind when he placed on his desk the reminder "The buck stops here." More often than not the President will be ignorant of many of the practices in his own administration, and his own values will never capture the executive branch completely. This, however, does nothing to change his obligation to exert the maximum control which time and the inertia of modern bureaucracy will permit.

Finally, I do not intend to suggest that the burden on the President to protect constitutional rights is ultimately any greater than it is for the other institutions of American government or for the least of us. Even if it were desirable, the President as one man would be incapable of such an awesome responsibility. What is needed is sound leadership which considers the interests of our traditional liberties as a part of national policy, not an easy reliance on the executive to govern liberty by institutional or personal legerdemain. The defense of constitutional rights is neither the most pressing presidential responsibility nor one that is solely his.

Although this study is not a systematic "survey" of presidential power as it relates to individual liberty, it should provide considerable evidence of the comprehensiveness of the President's responsibility. I hope that it will inspire further scholarly inquiry into what could not be discovered or discussed exhaustively.

The scheme of analysis falls into the traditional form: how the President, as chief legislator, chief administrator, chief executive, and leader of his party and the public, may protect and encourage respect for individual liberty. The prejudices lying behind this study are uncomplicated. They are the prejudices of a constitutionalist who believes that just as freedom must be protected by our foreign policy so too must the protection of constitutional rights be a persistent ingredient in the administration of affairs at home. When it is not, the essential substance of constitutionalism will suffer.

For those who have encouraged and contributed their insight to this inquiry, I wish to express a profound indebtedness; Clinton Rossiter, Robert E. Cushman, and Raymond English gave their invaluable support from the beginning. Thanks are due also for the grants-in-aid from the Fund for the Republic and the American Philosophical

Society, for the financial assistance from the Harry S. Truman Library Institute for National and International Affairs which made search in the Truman Library possible, and for the co-operation of the Trustees of Kenyon College. I am also grateful for a grant from the John L. Senior Endowment at Cornell University which enabled me to put the final touches on what appears below. Portions of Chapter VI have appeared in a slightly different form in my article "The Cold War Presidency," which was published by the Hansard Society for Parliamentary Government in a volume of essays, *Present Trends in American National Government* (London, 1960).

The imaginative archival assistance of Herman Kahn of the Franklin D. Roosevelt Library, Hyde Park, and Philip C. Brooks and James R. Fuchs of the Harry S. Truman Library, Independence, Missouri, led me to information which both confirmed and put in question my own presuppositions. Many friends and colleagues contributed valuable critical insight in conversations on this special problem of the presidency. I am especially indebted to Steven Muller, Robert J. Steamer, and H. Landon Warner for reading the manuscript in its rougher form and to my wife, Dorothy Seiler Longaker, who, together with Sarah, Richard, and Stephen, contributed to this result by their co-operation and patience. Many other persons gave their time in brief or extensive interviews; to them the study owes much of its substance. The reconstruction of fact and the conclusions are, of course, my own.

R. P. L.

Ithaca, New York
September 1960

x

Contents

The Presidency and Individual Liberties

"The committee, appointed the 9th instant, 'to consider and report under what title it will be proper for the Senate to address the President of the United States of America,' reported: 'That, in the opinion of the committee, it will be proper thus to address the President: *His Highness, the President of the United States of America,* and *Protector of their Liberties.'* " Annals of Congress, 1789

"If the Almighty Being who has hitherto sustained and protected me will but vouchsafe to make my feeble powers instrumental to such a result, I shall anticipate with pleasure the place to be assigned me in the history of my country, and die contented with the belief that I have contributed in some small degree to increase the value and prolong the duration of American liberty."
ANDREW JACKSON in his Protest to the Senate, 1834

"Excessive security . . . can be as dangerous as inadequate security. Excessive security brings normal administrative operations to a standstill, prevents the interchange of ideas necessary to scientific progress, and—most important of all—encroaches on the individual rights and freedoms which distinguish a democracy from a totalitarian country. Every proposal for new internal security laws, therefore, should be carefully scrutinized not only from the standpoint of how much it will add to national security but also from the standpoint of the other considerations noted above, and particularly the last."
HARRY S. TRUMAN to Attorney General McGrath, 1950

"One of the fundamental concepts of our constitutional system is that it guarantees to every individual, regardless of race, religion, or national origin, the equal protection of the laws; thus those of us who are privileged to hold public office have a solemn obligation to make meaningful this inspiring objective. We can fulfill that obligation by our leadership in teaching, persuading, demonstrating, and enforcing the law."
DWIGHT D. EISENHOWER in his State of the Union Message, 1959

I

Constitutional Rights
and the Modern Presidency

THE crisis of constitutionalism in the mid-twentieth century is only one episode in the long history of liberty, but it may well be the decisive one. Whether constitutionalism will endure depends not alone on military power, science, or even a spirited national resolve, but on the ability of the United States, as one democratic nation, to apply ancient principles of constitutional restraint in the presence of new conditions and to assimilate the interests of the constitutionally underprivileged into a more perfect system of equal rights. The compelling forces at work in the world, the forces of racial antagonism and aspiration, of the maximizing of governmental power and the minimizing of restraints, have already affected the older social and constitutional patterns, and they may be expected to do so for many years to come. They have heaped complexity and confusion on styles of belief and behavior which were once the "self-evident" principles of a calmer constitutional period.

The responsibility for revitalizing, broadening, and applying the best of the American constitutional tradition in a rapidly changing situation is one shared by all American institutions, both public and private; and not the least of these are Congress and the judiciary. But the nature of the executive in the modern security state and the popular roots of the office make the role of the presidency one of paramount importance. The evidence lies in the shower of issues intimately related to constitutional liberty which have fallen persistently on the White House since 1940. Little Rock, civil rights legislation, loyalty-security, desegregation, and discrimination are all major aspects of the history of liberty in the United States while, significantly, they constitute a small but weighty portion of presidential policy problems since World War II. Both the marked advances and the dismaying retrogressions in this realm owe as much to the White House as to any other American institution.

Perhaps this has always been so. In the early days of the Republic, John Adams encouraged and abetted the Alien and Sedition Acts, while Jefferson contributed to their demise; at the same moment Lincoln brought about the end of Negro slavery, he trampled on constitutional rights in order to save the Constitution; and Woodrow Wilson presided over the suppression of individual rights during the First World War in an effort to secure freedom for millions abroad. There are many other scattered instances in the history of the presidency which further illustrate that nothing is completely without precedent. Andrew Jackson threatened to dispatch troops to uphold the law against a recalcitrant Southern state; Theodore Roosevelt broke the color line in White House social propriety; Warren G. Harding used the pardoning power to mitigate some of the injustices of World War I. There is a familiar ring to it all. Constitutional issues may have their fashions, but under the surface they remain much the same. Similarly, the fundamental problem of political power seldom changes; power is used responsibly or it is misused. Nonetheless, those two insistent companions of the Cold War and social change, internal security and equal rights, have put the axiom *Plus ça change, plus c'est la même chose* to a severe test. One major consequence has been to elevate the presidency to a position of power and responsibility never quite experienced before. Where once presidential involvement with constitutional rights was brief and intermittent, it is now direct, inevitable, and enduring.

The Roots of Presidential Responsibility

Why is presidential contact unavoidable? At one time a President could afford to be neutral or indifferent in controversies over the Bill of Rights; now the issues seem to compel presidential attention. Futhermore, they promise to do so for many presidential generations. Because Presidents tend to share the nation's growing self-conscious interest in individual liberty, no doubt they will find it difficult to remain aloof. Most men have been stirred, one way or the other, by the vigor of attacks on liberty at home and abroad—by Nazi and Communist ideology or by native superpatriotism and racial prejudice. The issues have been magnified and perhaps clarified by a war and a Cold War fought in their defense and also by the subtle yet pervading influence of libertarian groups and the educational effect

3

of a long cycle of Supreme Court decisions.[1] A President, as other men, will find it difficult to avoid some reaction to this ferment; as with all men in public life, his opinion will be sought. The sustained effort to elicit some personal statement from President Eisenhower on the morality (or immorality) of the Supreme Court's desegregation decision or about Senator McCarthy's charges of disloyalty within the government bears witness to this.

But in recent years there have been factors other than personal inclination or disinclination which intrude from the world outside the White House to hasten presidential involvement. Of the many problems facing America at mid-century few are or have been as uninviting as the impact of the Cold War on constitutional rights or the trauma associated with evolving Negro aspirations. Both have political, administrative, and moral implications which draw a President to his responsibility. Not since the days of Reconstruction has the nation been pressed to shift deeply rooted social patterns with "all deliberate speed"; never before has the nation faced a security emergency of indefinite duration.

The unparalleled strain which the Cold War has placed on constitutional rights is reflected in the unsettled state of most American political beliefs and institutions. Convictions about the separation of powers, for instance, or the powers of Congress, executive agencies, and the presidency itself, have been shaken. Congressional power has waned while the President's responsibilities as international

---

[1] See the stimulating essay by John P. Roche, "American Liberty: An Examination of the 'Tradition' of Freedom," in Milton R. Konvitz and Clinton Rossiter, eds., *Aspects of Liberty* (Ithaca, 1958), 158–159.

leader have grown; as for the separation of powers, the Cold War's hunger for speed and secrecy in the execution of foreign policy have rendered "the triple complications" of the Founding Fathers archaic; and the executive branch, once a more simple administrative entity, frequently gives the appearance of a self-sufficient Roman Empire. Unavoidably, because the President is the primary guardian of security, the real impact of constitutional rights has taken place within the executive's domain. There, in the first instance, rights may be harmed or protected. A President is confronted by the rich ambiguities of a Cold War stretching into infinity—a situation which encourages administrative habits of mind which neither war alone nor peace alone would produce. In war, security must prevail; in peace, security is peripheral. In a Cold War liberty and security are jumbled together, each voicing claims to respect.

Almost invariably security gets the best of the initial argument, for, it is asked, who can "gamble" with the survival of the nation? The administrative reply, more often than not, is to do what appears to be safe and certain, and a zealous emphasis on security gives the illusion of being just that. Because the ambiguous emergency has no termination, the military police aspects of government are exalted, and a security-oriented bureaucracy becomes entrenched. With the major share of executive energy devoted to counteracting the threat of communism, executive personnel tend to accept a presumption against risk and a presumption for security as they pursue their own narrow function. To this is added the eternal tendency of a bureaucracy—which increases in intensity as it increases in size—to depersonalize the objects of administration and to expand the secrecy

5

of its operations. As a result, bureaucratic habits and the administrator's self-interest, stimulated by congressional and popular clamor, too frequently dictate that conformity and security shall take precedence over constitutional safeguards. Thus, passports have been denied on grounds unclear to the administrator himself, documents with only a trace of security content have been withheld from the press and the public, and employees have been discharged from the government service for reasons quite unrelated to their present capacity to serve the government creatively. The inherent conventions and conformities of an expanding bureaucracy are compounded by the deep-seated security consciousness of the Cold War. Where once the government reacted to an emergency by imposing temporary restrictions on the Bill of Rights, now both the restrictions and the sense of emergency are continual.

Inevitably then, where there is Cold War policy, there will be a threat to constitutional rights; and where there is Cold War policy, there will be the President. He may succumb to the restrictive tendencies of his own bureaucracy or, alert to an obligation to the Bill of Rights, attempt to counteract them. Either way, the influence of the presidency will be felt. For every attempt to disengage the White House from decisions affecting individual rights will reinforce the discretionary powers of those lower in the bureaucracy where the problem cannot be avoided.

Similarly, the hard necessities of a Cold War have produced an unavoidable presidential responsibility toward Negro rights. Few can deny that events in Mississippi reverberate in Asia or that a government which frowns on race riots in South Africa may easily justify complacency toward its own race problem. Indeed, shadows anywhere on

6

the figure of American Liberty—cast by a conformist atmosphere, violations of free speech, or hysteria—will damage the image of America in foreign eyes and thus undermine the President's power as a leader abroad. Security, liberty, and equality are close associates and not always incompatible ones. The congressional hysteria over "loyalty" in the mid-fifties probably damaged American security, and the spate of "book burnings" by American agencies abroad were viewed as crucial flaws in American constitutionalism. But nowhere has the distance between the constitutional dream and social reality been more noticeable than in American race relations. In a world ready to scoff at the pretensions of American leadership, the unpunished murderers of Negro citizens, revilers of Negro school children, or the bombers of churches involve the security of the nation in their own delinquencies. President Eisenhower's response to the racial clash over school integration in Little Rock in 1957 was, by his own admission, as much related to sensitive world opinion as the necessities of law enforcement. As he declared in an address to the nation during that crisis:

At a time when we face grave situations abroad because of the hatred that communism bears toward our system of government based on human rights, it would be difficult to exaggerate the harm that is being done to the prestige and influence, and indeed to the safety, of our nation and the world. . . . Our enemies are gloating over the incident and using it everywhere to misrepresent our whole nation.[2]

This message seemed to herald an end to presidential indifference to affairs once considered largely local. Whatever

[2] *New York Times,* Sept. 25, 1957.

a President's judgment may be about the immorality of segregation or discrimination, a nationally shared interest in national security has come to demand unremitting attention to events which may blot the record of American constitutionalism among the President's overseas constituency.

The imperatives of America's overseas position are matched by the imperatives of public and party expectations at home. Americans now take the presidential presence for granted whenever a major national problem appears, whether to repair the social and economic damage of a flood, drought, or recession, or to meet a crisis in foreign policy or education, or even to lift the moral tone of the nation. As the people have come to see the presidency as their office, they have heaped on it the burden of their expectations. These expectations in the realm of First Amendment freedoms have run the course from stopping subversion to stopping hysteria, with different publics asking the President to do different things. Whereas his action will antagonize some groups, indifference will antagonize all. As for Negro rights, public expectations are less complicated. Negroes demand presidential intervention against discrimination while those opposed seek presidential quiescence. In this case, the price of indifference may be the loss of the Negro vote, which is now of crucial political significance.

Some date the political coming of age of the Negro in the defeat of Judge Parker's nomination to the Supreme Court, partly through the efforts of the NAACP, in 1931.[3] In view of the ease with which President Roosevelt muted

[3] Walter White, *A Man Called White* (New York, 1948), 104–110.

the civil rights demands of Negroes during the 1930's this date is probably a decade too soon. Roosevelt, apparently by conscious decision, subordinated the direct civil rights program of Negro groups to the indirect benefits of economic and social gain of the New Deal and later to the world-wide struggle for liberty in World War II.[4] Wendell Willkie's attention to the Negro vote in 1940 along with the improved organizational tactics of the Negro leaders in the late 1930's finally excited specific White House attention. Organizational pressure, in particular the threatened march on Washington by 10,000 Negroes, obtained from a reluctant President limited but significant adjustments in discrimination against Negroes in the armed services and in hiring for defense production.[5] Negroes discovered close political friends in the White House. What had been, thirty years before, a problem of local tactics had become by 1940 a crucial question of national political strategy. The time was past when a White House greeting to a visiting Negro delegation could take the form of "What do you boys want?"[6]

[4] Interview with Mrs. Franklin D. Roosevelt, June 4, 1958.

[5] White, *A Man Called White*, 187–188; Herbert Garfinkel, *When Negroes March* (Glencoe, Ill., 1959), 16ff. During the 1940 campaign Stephen Early, the President's press secretary, kicked a Negro policeman in New York. The embarrassment to the Democrats and to the President was so great that the President is said to have refused to speak to Early for days.

[6] A Negro leader protested about a reception of this sort in a letter to the President's press secretary on Aug. 23, 1933 (Franklin D. Roosevelt Papers, Roosevelt Library, Hyde Park, N.Y.). And in 1940 aspiring politicians would not write to friends as Franklin D. Roosevelt did during the Washington race riots in 1919, "With your experience in handling Africans in [Little Rock!] Arkansas, I think you had better come up here and take charge of the Police Force" (F.D.R. to Joseph R.

9

Thus, the question is not whether to meet with Negro groups, or to introduce legislation, or to act administratively for their benefit; the problem now is one of timing rather than substance, for the coin of this realm of individual liberty is electoral support. Even so, for the presidency the immediate political power of the Negro voter in crucial urban areas is complicated by the fundamental social change which their demands entail. The political pressure cannot be alleviated by the chief executive's delivering a package of legislative and administrative benefits—as it can be, at least momentarily, with farm, labor, or business groups— but only by a persistent attack on the social basis of the Negro complaint. The range of possible political mistakes in such a situation is great, for the nature of our governmental system denies the President the power to do all that this specific minority group asks. On occasion, emphatic presidential intervention may be called for against this (or any other) minority when, by virtue of its political power and the memory of its own suffering, it is tempted to infringe on the constitutional rights of others. In any case, cautious, constructive leadership may easily be misconstrued as faintheartedness by those struggling to escape a heritage of denial.

But if for no other reason than the blunt fact of the electoral vote in New York City, Chicago, Philadelphia, and, in the years ahead, the South, the political President or presidential hopefuls cannot avoid forceful leadership in civil rights. Harry Truman was aided in 1948 by the defection of the Dixiecrats, Senator Eastland was an in-

Hamlem, July 26, 1919, cited in Frank Freidel, *Franklin D. Roosevelt: The Ordeal* [Boston, 1954], 30).

10

valuable symbol for the Republicans in 1956, and, in 1960, both parties attempted to outbid each other by adopting civil rights planks which were unprecedented in their disregard for Southern discontent and equally unprecedented in the scope of their election-year promises for Federal action in support of civil rights. Despite the predominant Negro loyalty to the Democratic party since the 1930's the inherent instability of this loyalty requires careful political attention, whichever party is campaigning, whichever party is in office. In congressional election years the issue may become localized temporarily and national leadership appear faint; but in presidential election years the ardor, for sound political reasons, will return. The elementary rule of American politics that a Southerner is an unacceptable nominee for the highest office is sufficient testimony to the force of this calculation. But if a Southerner is nominated for the presidency in the years to come, he too will have to take notice, as did Senator Lyndon Johnson when he became an aspiring presidential candidate and a vice-presidential nominee in 1960, of the connection between his record on civil rights and his chances of victory or defeat. To say this is to mark the change. President Wilson could afford to maintain a cool distance between himself and Negro groups; Hoover remained aloof in what came to be called "the lily-white White House"; and Franklin D. Roosevelt never released his full power in a legislative struggle over civil rights. In sum, presidential candidates and Presidents must now take Negro demands seriously or place their party in political jeopardy. Furthermore, Presidents must respond to Negro aspirations or face the prospect of damaging American prestige abroad. Similarly,

Cold War administration assures that a President will become involved in the intricacies of due process of law and the Bill of Rights. When a President acts in the defense of constitutional rights, or against them, whether from considerations of foreign policy, constitutional morality, or politics, he will find that his posture is frequently decisive. For added to his burden are the deficiencies in positive action by Congress or the courts when they stand alone.

The Limitations on Congress and the Judiciary

What the national legislature and the Federal judiciary are unable or unwilling to do may create a hiatus which only the national executive can fill. For those born into a tradition of legislative guardianship of individual liberties and a generation accustomed to reliance on the Supreme Court this may seem to elevate the executive unduly. It is, however, the present constitutional reality. Not the least important is the fact that the laws can be executed only with presidential co-operation. Furthermore, in recent years the body of Federal law affecting individual liberties has come to include a profusion of statutes and court decisions in the internal security field and civil rights. Thus as liberty is increasingly absorbed into the legalism of the modern state, the executive becomes the central figure in determining the quality of the law's application. As chief executive a President may set the tone of enforcement and, in so doing, will have an inevitable impact on the rights of individuals affected by the law.

Although these facts alone reduce the power of Congress and the Federal judiciary to protect liberty unaided, there are still other inherent limitations. The loyalty of Congress is largely local; and where legislative sentiment attempts to break the ties of particularism, it confronts the armor of procedural complications, filibuster, and committee autonomy which protects the substance of the national legislature's fundamental localism.[7] The Supreme Court, on the other hand, is limited because its process is essentially reactive. The Federal judiciary cannot initiate cases or seek out violations of liberty but must choose from those cases appealed by others. It cannot take immediate action upon observing a violation of constitutional rights. Moreover, once it does act, in the carefully prescribed realm of "case or controversy," it cannot, except by implication, suggest alternatives. Its role is largely negative—reconciling, cautioning, and retarding the policies of the other branches and other levels of government. The Federal courts, in a word, possess "no self-starter,"[8] and, by definition, leadership cannot exist under circumstances of counteraction alone.

The element of time also limits the effectiveness of the judiciary as a guardian of liberty. Damage may be done to individual liberty months or years before the case reaches the Supreme Court, if it ever does. The "Attorney General's list," a potpourri cataloguing of "subversive organizations," had become an American institution before the Supreme Court questioned its legality in 1951. And when the Supreme Court finally limited the loyalty-security program, it could not undo, by affirming judicially a single claim made years

[7] See Ch. II for further discussion of this point.

[8] Albert P. Blaustein and Clarence C. Ferguson, Jr., *Desegregation and the Law* (New Brunswick, N.J., 1957), 39.

13

before, the damage done to a multitude of innocent individuals.[9] The executive, unlike the courts, may be able to avoid the original violation which breeds the case. Furthermore, the nature of executive power permits initiation where violations occur and allows the formulation of alternatives and positive leadership (whether by administrative action or adjudication) rather than the passive counteraction characteristic of the judicial process.

Where time and the nature of the judicial process itself do not establish limits, the Supreme Court finds still other limitations to impose. The Court, following its own canons of self-restraint, has used the weapon of narrow statutory construction to deter Congress and the executive rather than a finding of unconstitutionality. In only a few instances in recent years has the Court used the ultimate test of constitutionality where individual liberties were in question.[10] It has preferred the indirect and more conditional restraint of strict statutory construction. For example, the loyalty-security program was not declared unconstitutional but attacked obliquely (on the grounds that the Summary Suspension Act of 1950 confined itself to employees holding

[9] *Joint Anti-Fascist Refugee Committee* v. *McGrath*, 341 U.S. 123 (1951), and Robert H. Jackson, *The Supreme Court in the American System of Government* (Cambridge, 1955), 24–35; *Service* v. *Dulles*, 354 U.S. 363 (1956). As one writer has remarked of *Ex parte Endo*, a Japanese-American relocation case, "To those affected, Supreme Court reversal of arbitrary action can never be as satisfactory as proper action in the first place" (Bernard Schwartz, *The Supreme Court* [New York, 1957], 293).

[10] See, for example, *Toth* v. *Quarles*, 350 U.S. 11 (1955); *Trop* v. *Dulles*, 356 U.S. 86 (1958); *Kinsella* v. *United States*, 80 S. Ct. 297 (1960).

14

"sensitive" positions).[11] The Court, then, beyond requiring that certain procedural guarantees be met, is asking for little more than "the sober second thought" by Congress and the executive, while—for reasons of self-restraint—it refuses to interdict the programs altogether. A slight shift in administrative practice or new legislation may be all that is needed to overcome the low barrier erected by the judiciary. Judicial protection of individual liberties, as a consequence, may in many cases be only momentary; the burden falls heavily on the executive to resist harmful legislation and cure its own administrative malpractices.

Although it is losing some of its strength, judicial scrutiny is limited further by the doctrine of privilege. The doctrine originates in traditional judicial deference to the executive where national security is at stake and in an obscurely drawn distinction between a "privilege" and a "right." Two major uses of this concept should be emphasized. The executive, when fulfilling its unique obligation to national security, possesses an area of action privileged from judicial interference; and further, certain relationships between the individual and the government are in the nature of privileges rather than constitutional rights. Thus, there is no constitutional right to get information from the government, and there is no constitutional right to be employed by the government. An alien has no constitutional right to escape quick deportation, and (until recently) there was

[11] *Cole* v. *Young*, 351 U.S. 536 (1956). For an evaluation of the effectiveness of the Supreme Court in this field see C. Herman Pritchett, *The Political Offender and the Warren Court* (Boston, 1958), 48–52.

15

no constitutional right to obtain a passport for travel.[12]

As this partial list illustrates, and this is the moral, the doctrine of privilege presumes that there will be a minimum of judicial interference in areas where individual liberty is particularly susceptible to executive restraint. The courts have stepped in to enforce an increasing amount of procedural protection,[13] and the right to travel has been elevated above its one-time secondary status; but in no instances have the courts denied to the executive the substantive power to restrain. It is doubtful if the judiciary will ever shatter the core of the problem of privilege, that is, the power of the executive to withhold evidence and sources of evidence when the executive determines that disclosure might threaten national security. This is so even though Chief Justice Warren attacked a proceeding under the industrial security program partly because confrontation and cross-examination were denied in the program.[14] Consequently, the Court may require procedure which, in the absence of executive self-restraint, will be little more than the skeleton of liberty. The executive is still permitted wide discretion in personnel security programs; deportation of aliens has received only a glancing blow of salutary judicial attention; and wire tapping can continue apace although the harvest of this habitual government activity cannot be used as evidence in the courts. As for the free flow of information, the Post Office Department and the

[12] *Kent* v. *Dulles*, 357 U.S. 116 (1958), and *Dayton* v. *Dulles*, 357 U.S. 144 (1958). For an excellent discussion of the doctrine of privilege see Kenneth Culp Davis, "The Requirement of a Trial-Type Hearing," *Harvard Law Review*, 70: 193–280 (1956).

[13] Davis, "Trial-Type Hearing," 225.

[14] *Greene* v. *McElroy*, 360 U.S. 474 (1959).

Bureau of Customs have wide powers of suppression, virtually untouched by emphatically clear judicial restraints; and the power of the executive branch to withhold information from the public, in turn, has escaped judicial scrutiny. For good reason, then, one authority remarks, "When in reality there is so little opportunity for review, the importance of sound initial decisions is emphasized." [15]

In time of war judicial restraint is more easily understood, and one is tempted to agree with the charming frankness of Mr. Justice Davis in *Ex parte Milligan:*

During the late wicked rebellion, the temper of the times did not allow that calmness in deliberation and discussion so necessary to a correct conclusion of a purely judicial question. Then, considerations of safety were mingled with the exercise of power; and feelings and interests prevailed which are happily terminated. Now that the public safely is assured, this question, as well as others, can be discussed and decided without passion.

But even in peacetime the court sets itself areas of judicial noninterference. Thus, executive privilege, coupled with

[15] Walter Gellhorn, *Individual Freedom and Governmental Restraints* (Baton Rouge, 1956), 94. See, generally, *Roth* v. *United States,* 354 U.S. 476 (1957); Harold Cross, "The Myth of Executive Privilege," in *Congressional Record* (daily ed.), Aug. 20, 1958, App. 7448; and the same author's observation elsewhere that "amidst those whose babel of voices determine as a practical matter the answer to the problem [of executive secrecy], the justices of the United States Supreme Court and the judges of the inferior courts established by Congress are for the most part a band of silent men. When they have spoken they have commonly said in effect: 'We may not speak. An executive officer has exercised his discretion.' Far too often the answer must indeed depend 'upon the courtesy of the government and upon its notion as to the public policy' involved" (Harold Cross, *The People's Right to Know* [New York, 1953], 229).

17

the restraints imposed on the courts by the nature of the judicial process and the judiciary itself, helps to create presidential opportunity. Furthermore, criticism of the Supreme Court, both from the extreme right and the extreme South and from more restrained voices, will throw greater responsibility on the executive branch as judicial activism moderates in response to the attacks. Paradoxically, while congressional and executive inattention to individual liberties seems to have encouraged heightened judicial activism, diminished judicial activism will create a greater burden for President and Congress. Yet even under an activist judicial doctrine there is ample room and need for constructive presidential activity.

Some Historical Observations

The presidency has been forced into the field of civil and political rights by the Cold War and the political power of minorities as well as the inherent limits on the other branches of the national government. It is a situation without full rehearsal in the nation's past although it is not difficult to find illuminating examples of prejudice and temper, courage and sensitivity to constitutional rights in the earlier history of the presidency. John Adams, pre-eminent among American constitutionalists, stirred up public feeling to bring about the adoption of the Alien and Seditions Acts and helped to see to their irresponsible enforcement.[16] Thomas

[16] Adams did nothing to calm the zeal of Federal judges and prosecutors. By his rhetorical attacks on the French and the Jeffersonians, in fact, the President seemed to hurry them on. In written addresses to the people Adams condemned "malicious demagogues [who] excite jealousies, ferment prejudices, and stimulate animosities." And, though admitting they were few, he suggested that they be "humbled in dust." As Fisher Ames commented, "The answers of the President have

Jefferson, the spokesman for natural rights who meticulously pardoned the victims of John Adams' wounded pride, was not without rancor where his own political enemies were concerned.[17] As for Andrew Jackson, although he was the first President to express a specific obligation as the people's tribune to protect popular liberties, he nonetheless encouraged his Postmaster General to use administrative coercion in order to halt the distribution of abolitionist literature in the South.[18] Lincoln, as he freed the slaves and preserved

---

elevated the spirit, and cleared the filmy eyes, of the many." It was in such an atmosphere that several newspaper editors and members of Congress were indicted and convicted for offending a statute which prohibited words, written or spoken, which might bring the Federal government and the President "into contempt or disrepute; or to excite against them . . . the hatred of the good people of the United States" (Statutes at Large, I, 597. See James M. Smith, *Freedom's Fetters* [Ithaca, 1956], 92).

[17] As the President wrote to Governor McKean of Pennsylvania: "The federalists having failed in destroying the freedom of the press by their gag-law, seem to have attacked it in an opposite direction; that is by pushing its licentiousness and its lying to such a degree of prostitution as to deprive it of all credit. . . . This is a dangerous state of things, and the press ought to be restored to its credibility if possible. The restraints provided by the laws of the States are sufficient for this, if applied. And I have, therefore, long thought that a few prosecutions of the most prominent offenders would have a wholesome effect in restoring the integrity of the presses. Not a general prosecution, for that would look like persecution, but a selected one" (Jefferson to McKean, *Works of Thomas Jefferson* [Ford ed.; New York, 1905], 9: 451–452; see also Edward S. Corwin, *Liberty against Government* [Baton Rouge, 1948], 158).

[18] Jackson believed that ostracization would settle the issue. He wrote to Postmaster Kendall: "I have read with sorrow and regret that such men live in our happy country—I might have said monsters—as to be guilty of the attempt to stir up amongst the South the horrors of a servile war— Could they be reached they ought to be made to atone for this wicked attempt, with their lives. But we are the instruments of,

19

the Union, brought the country closer to dictatorship than at any time in the nation's history.

But of twentieth-century Presidents, Woodrow Wilson mixed the most ample portions of illiberality toward constitutional rights with his political liberalism. It is perhaps no more than a historical oddity now that Wilson, progressive and Virginian by birth, was a willing instrument in the extension of segregation in the Federal service.[19] Of greater

---

and executors of the law; we have no power to prohibit anything from being transported in the mail that is authorized by the law. The only thing that can be done is what you have suggested, verbally, to the postmaster in the city, *to deliver to no person these inflammatory papers,* but those who are really subscribers for them; and few men in society will be willing to acknowledge that they are encouraging by subscribing for such papers this horrid and most wicked proceedure; and when they are known, every moral and good citizen will unite to put them in coventry, and avoid their society. This, if adopted, would put their circulation down everywhere, for there are few so hardened in villainy, as withstand the frowns of all good men. . . . and in every instance the Postmaster ought to take the names down, and have them exposed thro the publik journals as subscribers to this wicked plan of exciting the negroes to insurrection and to massacre. This would bring those in the South, who were patronizing these incendiary works into such disrepute with all the South, that they would be compelled to desist, or move from the country" (Jackson to Amos Kendall, Aug. 9, 1835, in J. S. Bassett, *Correspondence of Andrew Jackson* [Washington, 1931], 5: 360–361; see also Clement Eaton, "Censorship of the Southern Mails," *American Historical Review,* 48: 266–280 [Jan., 1943].

[19] Postmaster General Burleson and Secretary of the Treasury McAdoo, abetted by members of Congress, apparently stimulated the President's segregationist sympathies. The President did not resist. As he explained, "I would say that I do approve of the segregation that is being attempted in several of the departments. I have not always approved of the way in which the thing was done and have tried to change that in some instances for the better, but I think if you were

significance for the Cold War presidency are the wartime prosecutions of radicals and the postwar Red Scare so effectively fueled by Wilson's Attorney General, A. Mitchell Palmer. The President can be forgiven much, for he at least warned Palmer not to "let the country see red" and opposed some of the most extreme proposals issuing from his administration, including one to permit the trial of civilians by military commissions within the United States.[20] His illness, too, coincided with the worst of the Palmer raids, while during the war he was no less affected than other Presidents by the compelling logic of *inter arma silent leges.* On the other hand, Wilson cannot be absolved of blame for the ritual patriotism enforced by the Federal executive in these years. He is, perhaps, especially to blame since, as a profound observer of government, he had anticipated the impact of modern war on liberty. On the eve of America's declaration of war against Germany, Wilson lamented to the editor of the *New York World:*

Once lead this people into war and they'll forget there ever was such a thing as tolerance. To fight you must be brutal and ruthless, and the spirit of ruthless brutality will enter into the

---

here on the ground you would see, as I seem to see, that it is distinctly to the advantage of the colored people themselves" (Wilson to H. A. Bridgeman, Sept. 8, 1913, quoted in Arthur S. Link, *Wilson: The New Freedom* [Princeton, 1956], 251). See also Kathleen L. Wolgemuth, "Woodrow Wilson's Appointment Policy and the Negro," *Journal of Southern History,* 24: 457–471 (Nov., 1958), and the same author's "Woodrow Wilson and Federal Segregation," *Journal of Negro History,* 44: 158–173 (April, 1959).

[20] For an excellent discussion of this aspect of Wilson's presidency see, generally, Harry N. Scheiber, *The Wilson Administration and Civil Liberties, 1917–1921* (Ithaca, 1960).

very fibre of our national life, infecting Congress, the courts, the policeman on the beat, the man in the street.[21]

The remarkable aspect of this accurate prediction is that the man who anticipated the result did little to counteract it, and in some respects encouraged the intolerance. Presidential speeches before and during the war abounded with references to hyphenates and Americanism, much beyond the needs of the day. He was virtually silent as he witnessed the attacks on liberty during the war and afterward. When magnanimity might have softened the assault on dissenters, the President refused to pardon Eugene Debs, who was then serving a prison sentence for his alleged seditious activities.[22] Although Wilson opposed the more extreme legislative proposals affecting free speech, he nevertheless gave his full support to other wartime legislation and in the postwar period proposed a peacetime sedition statute.[23] The antics of the Department of Justice and the Department of Labor in prosecutions for sedition and for deportation went unchecked by the President, even though there were strong antagonists to the dominant mood of hysteria within the departments themselves.[24] Many months before the postwar vendetta of Attorney General Palmer, postal censorship

[21] Quoted in John L. Heaton, *Cobb of "The World"* (New York, 1924), 206.

[22] Josephus Daniels, *The Wilson Era: Years of War and After* (Chapel Hill, 1946), 365.

[23] Scheiber, *The Wilson Administration and Civil Liberties*, 11–28, 53.

[24] *Ibid.*, 42–43. For the conflict between Palmer and the Department of Labor see Zechariah Chafee, *Free Speech in the United States* (Cambridge, 1946), 214–215.

of innocuous literature had become commonplace and Federal district attorneys busied themselves with eager prosecutions under wartime legislation. In most instances the evidence was spurious and the legitimate needs of security were quickly displaced by the ritual value of a multitude of convictions. Through it all, as one commentator concludes, the President may have "blanched but he didn't intervene." [25]

There are many lessons in the Wilsonian experience, among them his disregard for the activity of his own administration during the war period, when presidential admonition and careful use of the appointing and removal power could have transformed administrative slashing into controlled prosecution related to the winning of the war. In his rush to make the world safe for democracy Wilson gave little attention to the domestic substance of that democracy which he was waging war to preserve, an experience which Cold War Presidents might well ponder. The postwar experience was no different, although at that time silence was imposed by an act of God. Nevertheless, the silence of Wilson's illness is as instructive as the silence of his disregard. Only the President could have counteracted the explosive mixture of Attorney General Palmer's zeal and political ambition, and only the President could have controlled the outpourings of the executive branch which reinforced the nation's insecurity and intolerance. The consequences of presidential inattention to personal liberties throughout the period of the war and its aftermath con-

[25] Eric F. Goldman, *Rendezvous with Destiny* (New York, 1953), 254–255.

tained the lesson of an emerging presidential responsibility.

What is most striking about Wilson's response is its contrast with the actions of two masters of wartime invasion of constitutional rights, Abraham Lincoln and Franklin D. Roosevelt. The Wilsonian reaction lacks the humanity, the self-doubt, and the declarations of necessity associated with the other two comparable periods of crisis. During the Civil War and World War II, invasions of individual liberty, when they came, were severe but were never marked by presidential indifference, nor did they lapse into crusades for ideological conformity. Presidential decisions were made reluctantly with a sense of the competing values at stake. There were, as well, conscious attempts to control the effects of the programs. In a word, constitutionalists may find evidence on both sides which may begin to justify the wholesale withdrawal of the writ of habeas corpus by President Lincoln or President Roosevelt's approval of the evacuation of Japanese-Americans from the West Coast in 1942. But the character and extent of prosecutions under the Wilson administration violate even the most flexible canons of crisis leadership.

To understand the relatively enlightened character of the repression of constitutional rights by Lincoln and Roosevelt is not to pass favorably on the wisdom of their decisions. Violations of individual liberties there were, and they were presidentially induced. Lincoln, struggling against disloyalty in the North as well as the South, suspended habeas corpus and in some areas of the country ordered the trial of civilians by military tribunals. Arbitrary arrests were made by the thousands, and the victims, far from the scene of war, were frequently denied the benefit of a speedy civil trial. In a proclamation which one authority calls "a perfect platform for despotism" [26] Lincoln commanded:

Now, therefore, be it ordered, first, that during the existing insurrection, and as a necessary measure for suppressing the same, all rebels and insurgents, their aiders and abettors, within the United States, and all persons discouraging volunteer enlistments, resisting militia drafts, or guilty of any disloyal practice affording aid and comfort to rebels against the authority of the United States, shall be subject to martial law and liable to trial and punishment by courts-martial or military commissions; second, that the writ of *habeas corpus* is suspended in respect to all persons arrested, or who are now or hereafter during the rebellion shall be imprisoned in any fort, camp, arsenal, military prison, or other place of confinement by any military authority or by the sentence of any court-martial or military commission.

The severity of the proclamation was lightened somewhat by the magnanimity of the President, but this spirit did not always guide his subordinates.

Much the same can be said of censorship during the Civil War. Lincoln was generally cautious in silencing the dissident voice of the press. Nevertheless, by controlling telegraph lines and censoring the mails and by outright military imprisonment of editors well beyond the combat areas, his subordinates attempted rigorous though unsystematic controls.[27] The President was surprisingly tolerant of press attacks on the administration. He also intervened in a hap-

[26] Wilfred E. Binkley, *President and Congress* (New York, 1947), 121. For the full text of the proclamation see James D. Richardson, *Messages and Papers of the Presidents* (Washington, 1899), 6: 98.

[27] See, generally, J. G. Randall, *Constitutional Problems under Lincoln* (Urbana, 1951), chs. vi–viii, xix.

hazard fashion to soften the effects of military trials of civilians. David Davis describes one such instance:

When Joseph E. McDonald went to Lincoln about those military trials and asked him not to execute the men who had been convicted by the military commission in Indiana he answered that he would not hang them, but added "I'll keep them in prison for a while to keep them from killing the government." [28]

Rough presidential justice, even if one accepts the necessity for executive interference with individual liberties in a crisis, is no substitute for orderly appeals, just administration, and the rudiments of due process of law which ought to survive even in war.

That orderly administration is, in turn, not a substitute for a policy unsound in conception is apparent in the emergency decision of Franklin D. Roosevelt in the early days of World War II to remove 120,000 Japanese-Americans from their West Coast homes. Not only hindsight but also evidence in hand at the time indicates that there was no convincing military case for the evacuation. Despite the presence of a deeper sense of the rule of law than one finds in the Civil War violations, imagined security needs overran any considerations of the profound individual price to be paid by the evacuees.[29]

[28] David Davis to William H. Herndon, Sept. 10, 1866, cited in David M. Silver, *Lincoln's Supreme Court* (Urbana, 1956), 235.

[29] Jacobus tenBroek *et al., Prejudice, War, and the Constitution* (Berkeley, 1954), ch. iii. Respect for the rule of law and civilian control ran into serious military obstacles in Hawaii. Until Secretary Ickes and others in Washington found the issue, all criminal law was under the control of military courts. The military held doggedly to their jurisdiction long after a threat of invasion had passed. See J. Garner Anthony, *Hawaii under Army Rule* (Stanford, 1955).

Although the evacuation of the Japanese-Americans occasioned heated discussions between departments in the administration, it received full presidential support. The opposition of the Department of Justice (including the FBI) was overwhelmed by the insistence of the military departments and President Roosevelt's easy surrender to this advice.

This executive invasion of constitutional rights was excused as a measure for preventing sabotage or a fifth column (a phrase very popular in those years) in the event of a Japanese attack on the West Coast. Some contended that the safety of Japanese-Americans required the evacuation because of steadily rising anti-Oriental sentiment in California. The last argument was based on fact; it is clear in retrospect, however, that the others were not. No incidents of sabotage can be traced to the mere presence of a concentrated Japanese-American population, and even before the evacuation began, the best military intelligence refused to accept an invasion of the West Coast as a possibility.[30]

This information was available to the President yet he succumbed to the excited concern of the Department of War and the importunings of the West Coast delegation in Congress. The matter was apparently discussed in cabinet meetings and with the President on other occasions by those who considered the move unwise. That part of the Roosevelt legend is unfounded which assures us that the President was too busy to consider the implications of his

[30] Anthony, *Hawaii under Army Rule*, 288–293; and see Justice Murphy's dissent in *Korematsu* v. *United States*, 323 U.S. 214, 241 (1944).

decision authorizing the evacuation. An army historian recounts:

The President told the War Department secretaries to go ahead and do anything they thought necessary under the circumstances. "We have carte blanche to do what we want to as far as the President's concerned," Mr. McCloy informed Colonel Bendetsen immediately after the White House conference. The President specifically authorized the evacuation of citizens. In doing so he observed that there probably would be some repercussions to such action, but said that what was to be done had to be dictated by the military necessity of the situation. Mr. Roosevelt's only reported qualification was "Be as reasonable as you can." [31]

In administrative fact and constitutional law, then, the decision was the President's. It was a coldly calculated priority of Dr. Win-the-War, as Roosevelt called himself, which fortunately did not set an administrative pattern for further suppression of individual liberty. Thus, there was no executive campaign for ideological conformity reminiscent of the Wilson administration, and criminal prosecutions were kept to a minimum.[32] John Adams, whose hypersensitivity to criticism was partly responsible for the Alien and Sedition Acts, could not have tolerated the personal attacks which President Roosevelt endured rather than

[31] Draft manuscript, "The United States in World War II: Western Hemisphere," vol. 2, ch. vi, "The Army and Japanese Evacuation," by Stetson Conn, pp. 39, 61.

[32] During World War I, over 2,000 persons faced prosecution; approximately 1,000 of them were convicted. In World War II only one periodical was suppressed—Father Coughlin's *Social Justice*—and there were relatively few prosecutions (Scheiber, *The Wilson Administration and Civil Liberties*, pp. 46–47, 61–63; Zechariah Chafee, *The Blessings of Liberty* [Philadelphia, 1956], pp. 70, 79). See the *Annual Report of the Attorney General*, 1942, 1943, 1944.

censor the offending publications. As for the Japanese-Americans, the President was not forgetful, for their welfare was apparently a question of some concern in the White House.[33]

These facts do not hide the enormity of the exception on the West Coast. Similarly, the evacuation itself cannot be blamed, in the final assessment, on "the military." This violation of liberty by the executive branch, like other major violations in the history of the presidency, included the President as supreme participant in the decision making. Participant or not, in this case as in all others, the President will bear the historical burden for the errors of his subordinates.

Some Presidents have benefited from reflection on the mistakes of their predecessors. President Roosevelt, remembering the hysteria of the Wilson era, apparently appointed Francis Biddle as a guardian against the same constitutional illness. President Truman recalled the race difficulties which followed World War I when he established the Committee on Civil Rights in 1947; and with characteristic historical sense he ordered a study of the Alien and Sedition Acts in anticipation of his veto of the Internal Security Act of 1950.[34] Reflection on these events in the total history of the presidency may alert a President to the variety of threats to

[33] Interview with Mrs. Franklin D. Roosevelt, June 4, 1958. The President was responsible in part for an inspection trip of relocation camps by Mrs. Roosevelt.

[34] Memorandum for Clark Clifford by Stephen J. Spingarn, April 6, 1949, Harry S. Truman Papers, Truman Library, Independence, Mo. Those close to President Roosevelt had the impression that the appointment of Francis Biddle was made partly because he believed that Biddle would avoid some of the excesses associated with World War I (interview with Benjamin V. Cohen, April 14, 1958).

constitutional rights in the nation's past. But, by and large, these scattered incidents are inadequate for the construction of a contemporary theory of responsibility.

Rather, a President may draw upon the deep heritage of the presidency and constitutional authority. The formulation, reinforced by continued White House experience, originates in the obligatory clauses of the Constitution and the ideas of the strong presidency associated with Jackson, Lincoln, Wilson, and both Roosevelts. Specifically, the theory of obligation combines the oath of office with the popular source of presidential responsibility and power. The former is found in the Constitution itself, the latter in the history of the presidency. The President is obliged by his oath of office to "preserve, protect, and defend the Constitution"; he is commanded by the example of Jackson to act as the tribune and "direct representative of the American people" and by Lincoln to serve as the conscience of the community.[35] The theories of Franklin D. Roosevelt and Woodrow Wilson direct the President toward the stewardship of enduring popular interest by transforming the office, in Wilson's words, into "the vital place of action" within the government and American society. The final dimension appears in Franklin D. Roosevelt's charge to Presidents to meet the challenges of the day with moral leadership. When the challenge embraces the shock of desegregation and the struggle to preserve traditional freedoms among the shifting pressures of the Cold War, an inert President may seriously impair the liberty which he is under oath to defend. As Roosevelt wrote soon after his first election:

[35] Richardson, *Messages and Papers of the Presidents*, 3: 90.

The Presidency is not merely an administrative office. That is the least of it. . . . It is preeminently a place of moral leadership. All of our great Presidents were leaders of thought at times when certain historic ideas in the life of the nation had to be clarified. . . . That is what the office is . . . a superb opportunity for re-applying, applying in new conditions, the simple rules of human conduct to which we always go back.[36]

The theoretical obligation carries with it, of course, the subsidiary constitutional power to see to the faithful execution of the laws, the techniques of legislative leadership and administrative control, and the function of party leadership and direction of public opinion. But all are secondary instruments designed to activate the vital merger between the oath of office and the popular and national character of the presidency. The oath is to "preserve, protect, and defend" a Constitution which embodies in its system of restraints and power the liberties of the community which the President represents.

Conclusion

How a President will act when constitutional rights move into his span of authority will depend on circumstances and his personality. He may either damage or restrict them or act positively to find a solution in their favor. But the once wide zone of choice, where avoidance and neglect were possible without destructive results, has virtually disappeared. The theory of the modern presidency and its capacity for action, the imperatives of domestic and international politics, and the unique institutional position of the executive in the American system, all push the

[36] *New York Times*, Nov. 13, 1932.

31

President increasingly toward constant involvement with individual liberties. His choice today is between making the executive branch either a participant in the protection and unfolding of liberty or, equally, through inaction and executive insensitivity, an agent in its decline.

Whether the President will take an affirmative role and whether he will be effective depend on the infinite variables of American politics and the conditions of leadership in a constitutional state. The character and quality of presidential leadership are typically determined by factors which accident or design bring together at a given moment of history. Crisis or emergency will diminish presidential interest in individual liberties and, correspondingly, extend the limits of permissible restrictions on constitutional rights. The public mood—and the way in which the President influences and interprets it—is of vital importance in determining the degree of presidential effectiveness. Questions of political advantage or fear of partisan reprisal are as relevant to problems of individual liberty as the constitutional values themselves. Few executive decisions are untouched by the consideration of the immediate or ultimate political consequences. The attitude of the individual President, both toward his office and its powers and toward the rights of others, is, of course, crucial. All are relative to time, personality, and situation. What is constant is the inevitability of presidential contact and the existence of the instruments for presidential action.

II

Presidential Leadership in Congress

THE strident voices heard in Congress as it spoke of internal security in the 1950's produced an image in many minds of Congress as the pre-eminent violator of individual liberty. It is true that lesser men of great emotions have used the forum of Congress and their own demagogic talents to obstruct civil rights legislation and to give distorted publicity to their schemes for halting subversion in government and elsewhere. On the whole this image of Congress breaks radically with the ancient Whig view of the legislature as the immovable obstacle against executive inroads into the substance of liberty. Unfortunately, on too many occasions, the image has been the reality. McCarthyism, using the legislative process as a vehicle of expression, became a way of life for many Americans and inundated portions of the executive branch. The touch of other extremists has colored the national attitudes toward dissent and tolerance in immigration legislation, in attacks on the Supreme Court, and in the nation's postwar series of security statutes. Congress, if noise alone is representative of quality, has no reason to

33

be proud of the tumult or of the acrid legislative smoke and heat.

Nevertheless, perspective demands that any discussion of the individual liberties role of the President in Congress be preceded by recognition of the role of Congress itself. Historically, there have always been individuals in Congress who have spoken out in defense of individual liberty, either against the incursions of the executive branch or the national legislature itself. When the Senate censured Senator McCarthy, it echoed the best of a heritage of legislative protection of the Bill of Rights, a heritage which has been represented by voice if not vote in the opposition of individual members of Congress to the Alien and Sedition Acts, Negro slavery, and the hysteria which arose during the later years of the Wilson administration. The Black and La Follette investigations of violence in the labor field and of lobbying together with the more recent Hennings and Moss investigations of the misuse of power by the executive testify to the use of committees as defenders, not assailants, of constitutional rights. And, if for the moment the damage inflicted by recent investigating committees is discounted, Congress must receive credit for alerting a somewhat incredulous executive to the largely inconsequential but real Communist infiltration of portions of the executive branch in the 1930's and 1940's. It is no violation of constitutionalism to presume that a system of liberty can exist only in a responsibly secure state. The same investigating weapon that produced the worrisome anticonstitutionalism of Senator McCarthy has been and can be used in fruitful defense of individual liberties. All legislative oversight of the bureauc-

34

racy can, by accident or design, ferret out administrative violations of liberty.[1]

In addition, the same system of rules and committee structure that permits the emasculation of civil rights legislation and perpetuates through the law of seniority the dynastic power of committee chairmen is not a one-way, antilibertarian street. The system provides the occasion for individual resistance to executive proposals hostile to civil liberties and presupposes caution and attention to the claims of a minority. Senator Richard Russell, of Georgia, may sometimes speak the social language of past centuries, but in reminding the nation, admittedly for the wrong reasons, of the danger of full-steam majoritarianism, he refers to a sound constitutional heritage. Against urgent presidential requests committees and individual Congressmen observed the better formula of caution in delaying passage of stringent passport legislation; and the successful fight against a stream of wire-tapping proposals has been waged with the weapons of congressional obstructionism, as was one vigorous attack on the Supreme Court.[2] Congress has added, on

[1] The Subcommittee of the Committee on Government Operations of the House of Representatives (Moss Committee on Government Secrecy), the Subcommittee on Constitutional Rights of the Committee on the Judiciary of the Senate (Hennings Committee), and a series of excellent committee hearings on passport administration and the loyalty-security program are notable post-World War II examples of congressional investigations of executive misbehavior affecting individual liberties.

[2] A threatened filibuster by non-Southerners stopped the regrettable "pre-emption" attack on the Supreme Court in the closing hours of the session in Aug., 1958. See Arthur Krock in the *New York Times*, March 3, 1960.

occasion, to the severity of security legislation but, in turn, has softened the effect or refused passage of measures supported by the police agencies in the executive branch. In sum, against the nationwide demand for security over liberty in the 1950's and the political mileage for members of Congress who charged the executive with laxness toward communism stood legislative power which could be used to protect the individual against public and bureaucratic extremism.

In fact, then, both Congress and the executive have a stewardship over constitutional rights, while legislation harmful to individual liberties has been generated by both the executive and legislative branches. The restrictive statutes passed since 1940 are joint products. The loyalty-security program, the Smith Act, and the Communist Control Act (signed by a President who did not want to be outmaneuvered politically) are examples of a joint submission by President and Congress to the same forces. In other instances—in immigration legislation and the Internal Security Act of 1950 —there is a strong suggestion in the legislative background that presidential opposition was offset by an alliance of sympathy and interest between the President's own agencies and Congress. In most cases vigorous if ineffectual opposition or enthusiastic support has not been the exclusive property of one branch or the other.

A description of the President's legislative role in defending and promoting individual liberty is not, then, a pure proposition of a courageous chief executive standing guard against congressional opportunism. That this image is accepted by some is McCarthy's greatest disservice to his colleagues. Equally, to expect the President to act as full-time keeper of the congressional conscience is to put a burden on the executive that should be borne by Congress itself.

Executive Initiative in Congress

These facts notwithstanding, the institutional characteristics of the presidency make the President less susceptible than Congress to the type of constituent pressure and petty partisanship which have marked so much of congressional activity in the security field and in civil rights. The President is free from the parochialism which afflicts Congress, even though his agencies possess their own strong parochial loyalties. He is both responsive and responsible to a larger constituency than the individual Congressman and has means of commanding the attention of that constituency. The President can frequently afford to stand above the immediate pressures of an insistent majority or the pressure of a well-organized local minority because the force of the demand when it reaches the White House is diluted by the variety and the size of the nation. He can take the lead because Congress in all its heterogeneity and the public with its expectations look to the executive for guidance. If the President takes advantage of his position and is willing to use the various techniques of legislative leadership, he can exert a decided if not always decisive influence at crucial turning points in the legislative process.

Before these techniques are discussed, it is essential to recognize that the degree of presidential success will be determined by a host of unpredictable factors, among which will be the President's willingness to act affirmatively and his ability and determination to control the insular demands

37

of his own agencies. The political complexion of Congress —that is to say, whether or not a majority is inclined to agree with the President—is important. More significant is the part played by the personal political ambitions of key members of Congress and the administration in activating this majority. Both presidential initiative and the quality of congressional responses are, of course, tuned to a political key. Nothing indicates this more clearly than the different treatment accorded legislation affecting the First and Fifth Amendment freedoms and that affecting minority rights.

A positive congressional attachment to at least minimal Federal protection of Negro rights—excepting, of course, the Southern delegation—has been matched in the past by a dominant willingness to overrun traditional constitutional guarantees. If the President chooses a positive role to protect and promote both civil rights and civil liberties, congressional considerations of political advantage will in the one case serve him, in the other hamper him. In other words, when Congress deals with minority rights the predominant mood is for favorable consideration of legislation; when it deals with measures affecting the broader guarantees of the Bill of Rights, the mood can become one of imperceptive apathy or antagonism. This legislative schizophrenia can be explained only in political terms, and the pattern will not change until it becomes politically popular to be an ardent proponent of the Fifth Amendment, due process, and free speech. Had not the presidential election been impending in 1948 and 1952, the original loyalty-security program might have taken another form, the administration of the program might have been less frantic, and the glaring purity of bipartisan loyalism less blind and blinding. But for the maneuvering of a little band of Democrats, the Communist Control Act would not have passed in 1954 or have been signed, in all its mysteries, by the President. And, conversely, but for the presidential ambitions of Richard Nixon and Lyndon Johnson the new Civil Rights Acts of 1957 and 1960 might have been swallowed up in a leaderless Senate.

If partisan calculations are never absent from congressional or presidential consideration of individual liberty questions, the intensity of such calculations, nonetheless, differs in each branch of the government. Presidents are more inclined and able to act against what appears to be their immediate political interest—as the potential political risks in the establishment of the Truman Committee on Civil Rights and President Eisenhower's failure to support legislation in 1957 authorizing the Attorney General to initiate school desegregation suits illustrate. By taking advantage of this margin of extrapartisanship and the traditional weapons of his office, the President, if post-World War II experience is to be the guide, will find several highly limited choices open to him when individual liberties and legislative maneuver intermix. His success will depend on the current political situation, the reservoir of friendly or hostile public opinion, and the effectiveness with which the techniques of legislative obstruction (the filibuster, the rules of procedure, and committee imperialism) are used, either to protect or to diminish individual liberties. His leadership will be dulled or sharpened in each instance by the degree of cohesion and ties of interest between his own agencies and members of Congress. And all the intangibles of personality, shrewd timing, and the force of moral argument as well as congressional susceptibility to more earthy means of persuasion will have a part to play. According to the issue, the absence or presence of an election year will have an impact; and always the President's determination will be conditioned by the state of his competing obligations and his sense of legislative priorities.

What, then, is the range of presidential choice when restrictive measures are to receive legislative attention? Certainly in recent years presidential initiation of legislation has been more harmful than helpful, and outright presidential opposition to the more extreme measures, when it has come, has been largely ineffectual against a security-minded Congress. As long as the Cold War mood lasts, the President's immediate obligation would seem to be to restrain the legislative notions of his own agencies and Congress itself. Even the best executive proposals will tend to be swept away or twisted out of shape by a current of congressional loyalism. If a President is able to control the security impulses originating within the executive branch, it is conceivable, for example, that limited proposals to improve existing law in regard to wire tapping or passport procedures might escape the potentially more severe hand of Congress; but such leadership must be cautious and geared to the public mood and that of Congress and its committees. Unless strong libertarian sentiments on a given issue are at one with the configuration of power in Congress, the proposal may succumb to the strength of a more extreme congressional legislation. Until such a dominant sentiment is evident, the President's major legislative responsibility will be not to initiate but to counteract ideas originating in Congress or his executive departments.

As for Federal protection of minority rights, the picture

is again somewhat different. Here the political interests of many members of Congress and the President coincide with the passage of affirmative legislation. It is to be expected that the tempo of the President's legislative initiative will increase as political pressure from Northern voters intensifies and as the powers of Southern obstruction are gradually worn down. The complicity of a Texan, Senator Johnson, and his colleagues from North Carolina, Florida, Tennessee, and Texas in the modification of the filibuster rule in the first session of the 86th Congress was a sign that the South was turning from obstruction to carefully bartered compromise. Nevertheless, White House initiative will never be unencumbered. Abundant procedural mechanisms and mutually beneficial alliances with other political groups in Congress will remain to protect the Southern minority. Further, presidential legislative leadership will continue to be restrained by other factors; among these are reasonable doubts about the effectiveness of omnibus legislation in the field of civil rights or, if not this, the fear that a strong civil rights program will hinder rather than help progress in the South or jeopardize other presidential programs in Congress.

This last point is of fundamental importance. It seems to have been a common legislative technique to give only half-hearted support to civil rights legislation, such as FEPC legislation, in return for Southern co-operation in the passage of foreign policy or welfare measures, although such arrangements are obviously difficult to document. The shifting alliances between the conservative Republicans and the Democratic South or the Western Democrats and the Southern Democrats represent the same kind of bargain. Franklin D. Roosevelt, for all his personal sympathy for the Negro, "placed civil rights legislation down the list [of his priorities] because he did not want to lose Southern support in Congress for the overwhelming necessities of defense preparation." [3] Perhaps, too, as some claim, President Truman made only formal requests for FEPC legislation, at times foregoing real legislative leadership in return for Southern acquiescence, while he attacked civil rights problems by administrative means.[4] It is incontestable that the Korean war paralleled a period of legislative reticence for the presidency in civil rights. And undoubtedly one reason for the reluctance of the Eisenhower administration to fight for legislation implementing the Civil Rights Act of 1957 in the next session of Congress was the strategic distribution of Southerners on committees dealing with legislative priorities of the session: reciprocal trade, defense reorganization, and mutual security appropriations. On the other hand, new proposals and executive eagerness for Federal protection of Negro rights increased with the approach of the presidential elections of 1960. But even in election years the President's responsibility to accommodate sectional differences, not exacerbate them, as well as his interest in buying co-operation for the rest of his program in Congress will temper presidential initiative.

[3] Interview with Mrs. Franklin D. Roosevelt, June 4, 1958. See also Walter White, *A Man Called White* (New York, 1948), 168.

[4] That this was not always so is evident from the President's messages and speeches on civil rights legislation and data in the Official Files. See the Memorandum of Stephen J. Spingarn, July 5, 1950, reporting the President's request that his assistants attempt to get a maximum vote for cloture against the filibuster on FEPC (Harry S. Truman Papers, Truman Library, Independence, Mo.).

The New Civil Rights Acts

It may be that the passage of the Civil Rights Acts of 1957 and 1960 over Southern opposition marks a new era in executive initiative. These statutes indicate that Congress will give a sympathetic hearing to measures which are in harmony with deeply held national beliefs, that is to say, that all Americans should have the right to vote. Even Senator Russell in his bayonets-in-the-backs-of-Americans speech during the debates on the 1957 bill admitted that "the American people generally are opposed to any denial of the right of ballot to any qualified citizen." [5] On the other hand, the legislative history of the new Civil Rights Acts gives considerable evidence of the limitations on civil rights leadership by the President in Congress.

The 1957 bill, as passed, did not attack segregation in the schools or elsewhere; it merely affirmed the traditional and generally accepted American right to vote. One suspects that even its opponents were touched by the compelling democratic logic of the bill. This may account for the temperate quality of the debate in the Senate. It was only occasionally marred by the potlikker arguments of an earlier day or by radical statements of Southern conservatives who referred to the right party but the wrong century in comparing Chief Justice Warren to Thaddeus Stevens. In 1957 that section of the administration proposal which provided for the protec-

[5] *New York Times*, July 3, 1957. Note also the remarkable degree of concurrence by the Southern members of the Commission on Civil Rights with the Commission's recommendations and findings of fact about Negro voting in the South (*Report of the United States Commission on Civil Rights, 1959*).

43

tion of the Negro's right to vote was not open to attack on the grounds of "separate but equal," the "mixing of the races," or legislative radicalism. It rested on its intrinsic merit and became law because of this and an overwhelming, if not unique, confluence of events. For the first time in eighty-two years a civil rights proposal coincided with favorable national newspaper and organization sentiment and with the political ambitions of Senate leaders such as William Knowland, Richard Nixon, and Lyndon Johnson.

Together with this, the proposal received strong administration endorsement, once it was restricted to voting rights. In addition, there was the willingness of civil rights leaders and the South to compromise and save the filibuster from a strong reaction to their own intransigence. Just as in 1960, by means of timely concessions and procedural forays from well-entrenched positions, the South not only accomplished this but also narrowed the application of the original administration proposal.[6]

Because the primary focus of this study is on the executive branch, it is essential to investigate the role of the White House in the passage of this new civil rights legislation. The original administration proposal in 1957 provided for the use of the injunctive process in the Federal courts to protect, at the request of an individual or the Department of Justice, voting rights and other civil rights including desegregation in the public schools.[7] It also contemplated a tem-

[6] Howard E. Shuman, "Senate Rules and the Civil Rights Bill: A Case Study," *American Political Science Review*, 51: 955–975 (Dec., 1957). See also Anthony Lewis, "The Professionals Win Out over Civil Rights," *Reporter*, May 26, 1960, pp. 27–30.

[7] See the testimony of Attorney General Brownell, *Hearings before*

porary commission on civil rights to investigate problems in the field, together with the strengthening of the fragile Civil Rights Section in the Department of Justice by elevating it to division status under an Assistant Attorney General. After debate in the Senate, which became "so complicated that only a layman could understand it," a conference committee of the two houses of Congress acceded to Senate demands and deleted all but the clause protecting voting rights (watered down by a jury trial requirement) and the provisions for a commission and a new Civil Rights Division in the Department of Justice. In this process one of many sops to Southerners was to remove from the statutes at large a section authorizing the use of troops by the President in enforcing court decrees.[8]

The earlier emphasis on the limitations of presidential legislative leadership in the field of civil rights strongly suggests that not even President Eisenhower's unqualified and firm support of the original proposal would have assured its passage in full. The legislative destiny seemed to point to the changes which were made. In particular, the deletion of Part III of the bill (which authorized the Attorney General to request court injunctions to protect an undefined array of civil rights and the final inclusion of some jury trial provision in contempt proceedings to protect voting rights) was preordained. On the other hand, the vacillation and uncer-

---

the Subcommittee on Constitutional Rights of the (Senate) Committee on the Judiciary, 85th Cong., 1st Sess., pp. 1–44 (1957).

[8] The section repealed was 42 U.S.C. 1993 (1952), which did not affect other statutory and constitutional authority for the President to use troops. See Ch. IV.

tainty of presidential leadership made the task of his legislative lieutenants and the Department of Justice more difficult.

It is impossible to reflect on President Eisenhower's role in the struggle for civil rights legislation in 1957 without distinguishing between the President and his administration. The fight for a workable bill was characterized by a massive administrative effort modified by alternating presidential support and doubts. The President wanted a bill protecting voting rights, and he attempted to persuade members of both parties of the wisdom of such legislation. His Republican leader for this bill in the House of Representatives has remarked that on no previous occasion had he been associated with legislation "in which the White House took a more active part." [9] Legislative strategy was discussed with the President, and members of the administration took the fight to the floor of Congress. The tempo of presidential efforts to persuade reluctant and indifferent members of Congress was greater in the House than in the Senate; but a degree of presidential presence was felt in both houses.

In three or four instances presidential intervention determined the direction of the legislative journey. First, the fact that the initial civil rights proposal was given the dignity of an "Eisenhower" bill meant that the issue could not be sidestepped in Congress. Second, when the Southern argument for jury trials in all contempt cases involving voting rights seemed to be winning, the President stood firmly opposed. Third, when the House-Senate conference threatened to run either way with the jury trial amendment, he accepted a half-loaf compromise rather than lose a workable, though

[9] Interview with Kenneth Keating, April 15, 1958.

limited, statute. Finally, it can be argued that if politics is the art of the possible the President played the game well in centering national and press attention on the issue of Negro voting rights. Few Americans, Congressmen included, could deny the worthiness of this appeal for equal justice.

To this extent the President's involvement assured passage of the Civil Rights Act of 1957. Nevertheless, the over-all quality of his legislative leadership was marred by clumsiness and uncertainty. There was a notable absence of enthusiasm and force in presidential defense of the bill. Although never amounting to indifference, it betrayed doubt. This is reflected in the President's reversal of his support for the original administrative proposal after Senator Russell's attack on "the subtle cunning" of the drafters of Part III.[10] In addition, in his press conference the President undermined his own administration:

I personally believe if you try to go too far too fast in laws in this delicate field that has involved the emotions of so many millions of Americans, you are making a mistake. I believe we have got to have laws that go along with education and understanding, and I believe if you go beyond that at any one time, you cause trouble rather than benefit.[11]

The President's generalization has much to commend it, but it was hardly appropriate at that point in the legislative battle.

[10] *New York Times*, July 3, 1957.

[11] The President's press conference, July 17, 1957, in *Public Papers of the Presidents of the United States, Dwight D. Eisenhower*, 1957, p. 556. The President confirmed this attitude two years later. See his remarks before the National Press Club, Jan. 14, 1959, *New York Times*, Jan. 15, 1959.

Lack of enthusiasm was matched by the President's lack of knowledge of the bill. He seemed to be poorly briefed on the exact contents and the range of technicalities in the field of civil rights enforcement. When reporters inquired whether the President would be willing to accept a bill limited to the protection of Negro voting rights and not school desegregation, he responded: "Well, I would not want to answer this in detail, because I was reading part of that bill this morning, and there were certain phrases I didn't completely understand." [12] Senator Russell, in this case a Southerner in statesman's clothing, filled the gap in the President's knowledge during a meeting at the White House. It was at this point that the President and his household became publicly divided.

The White House lost the impetus of its original initiative because of such incidents. The atmosphere of halfhearted conviction surrounding the President's public statements about the importance of Part III and lack of knowledge were compounded by an absence of strong, co-ordinated presidential direction in the Senate. The President and his advisers, congressional leaders, and the Department of Justice were frequently at odds or out of phase with each other. The weakness is reflected in the Russell incident and the confusion which dominated the twists and turns of debate on the jury trial amendment. "Where is the White House on this?" became a recurring question mark over much of the debate.

Perhaps as damaging in the end was the President's per-

[12] The President's press conference, July 3, 1957, *Public Papers of the Presidents*, p. 521. He added, "I know what the objective was that I was seeking, which was to prevent anybody illegally from interfering with any individual's right to vote."

sistent effort to reassure the South that troops would never be used to enforce desegregation. In his failure to oppose the repeal of part of the United States code which authorized the President to use troops to enforce court decrees, he provided fuel for those who later claimed that the legislative intent was against the use of force. Together with this, his statement that "I can't imagine any set of circumstances that would ever induce me to send Federal troops into a Federal court and into an area to enforce the orders of a Federal court" and the rumored "over my dead body" remark when the question was discussed in the White House cast doubt on the President's determination to see that the laws would be enforced.[13] The lack of stern public commitment was felt in the school desegregation crisis in Little Rock a few weeks later.

These flaws in presidential leadership aside, the Eisenhower administration deserves a unique position in the legislative history of civil rights for its part in bringing about the passage of the first civil rights legislation since the Reconstruction period. The cumulative effect of the administration's drive in 1957 assured the passage of the bill, even though much of the original substance was drained from it. That it passed against the grain of previous congressional experience with civil rights legislation is further reason to commend the administration. The event suggested, however, that omnibus civil rights legislation is not within the realm of legislative policy—rather that legislative protection of Negro rights will appear only in small lots, each carefully circumscribed to deflect a direct assertion of Federal power.

[13] The President's press conference, July 17, 1957, *ibid.*, 134; Arthur Krock in the *New York Times,* July 21, 1957.

This legislative destiny was fully confirmed by the history of the Civil Rights Act of 1960.

After considerable delay and amidst an air of hesitancy, the Eisenhower administration proposed a seven-point civil rights program in 1960. Following the passage of the 1957 Act, the administration had taken the position that the legislation had to be tested in the courts and that a cooling-off period in the South was not without merit. Two minor proposals were made to strengthen the earlier statute,[14] but an apparent presidential reluctance to legislate broadly in the area of civil rights together with the fear of jeopardizing a profitable partnership between some Northern Republicans and the Southern Democrats restrained executive enthusiasm. Successive waves of political pressure and legislative clamor brought about a change. The obvious deficiencies of the 1957 statute and criticism of the administration by the Commission on Civil Rights joined with the urgencies of an election year to bring about the introduction of a full-scale administration program.[15] The administration avoided the

[14] For the administration proposals see the *New York Times*, Feb. 6, 1959.

[15] For the Commission on Civil Rights criticism see the *Report*, 1959, pp. 128–134. The Commission proposed a Federal "registrar" plan which would have empowered the President to appoint Federal officials to register Negro voters. Attorney General Rogers apparently had serious administrative and constitutional doubts about the plan; some commentators have suggested, further, that the administration did not want to frighten away the potential Republican vote in the South by supporting this method of direct intervention. Senator Johnson had seized the initiative in 1959 with his mild plan for the establishment of "conciliation" commissions in the South (*New York Times*, Jan. 21, 1959). The various proposals and problems associated with civil rights legislation were thoroughly discussed at a valuable conference at Notre Dame. See Harris Wofford, Jr., "Notre Dame Conference

controversial Part III (which in 1957 was proposed as a means for direct Federal intervention in school desegregation cases), thereby committing itself to a "moderate" approach, but it did support a new statutory provision for additional protection for voting rights by assisting Negroes to register, after complicated proceedings, with the help of local "referees" appointed by the Federal district judges. The program made it a criminal offense to bomb schools or churches or to obstruct court orders in desegregation cases by violence or threats of violence. The 1957 Act was to be amended by requiring the preservation of voting records, and the economic and social strain of desegregation was to be eased by special Federal grants of assistance to communities inaugurating school desegregation plans and by making provision for the education of the children of servicemen when state policy closed the schools near military bases.[16]

In characteristic fashion, the original proposals were whittled down by a combination of Southern legislative astuteness, the divisive effect of political maneuvering between various factions in the two political parties, and the maladroitness in the operations of the pro-civil rights forces which was carefully exploited by those wishing a severely restricted bill or no bill at all. It is difficult to evaluate the role of the White House except to say that the President once again concentrated his support on the voting aspects of the bill. His leadership brought many hesitant Republicans into line. But the directives emerging from the White House were frequently unclear and lacked the vigor to pull together a

---

on Civil Rights: A Contribution to the Development of Public Law," *Notre Dame Lawyer,* 35: 328–367 (May, 1960).

[16] See the *New York Times,* Feb. 6, 1959, Jan. 27, 1960.

divided Republican party and to resolve divisions within the administration itself. The executive capitulated too easily to pleas for compromise, while an aura of presidential "neutrality" on the question of civil rights and a reluctance to strain the conservative alliance between Northern Republicans and Southern Democrats were always in the background. Attorney General Rogers, who shaped the administration program, was hampered by these factors as well as hostile, election-year majorities in Congress. Above all, Senator Lyndon Johnson, through deftness and a keen sense of the minimum degree of "moderation" which Congress would accept, dominated the proceedings.

It is not surprising, then, that the Civil Rights Act of 1960 emerged as little more than a sister statute of the earlier act. Provisions for Federal aid to communities in the throes of desegregation and statutory authority for the President's Committee on Government Contracts were lost, and a major amendment to the voting protections of the 1957 Act, the so-called "referee" provision, was interlaced with enough procedural trip wires and ambiguity to make a decided increase in Negro voting under its provisions problematical at best. Nevertheless, small but significant amendments were added to ease the enforcement of the 1957 statute, and the referee provision itself promised a slow and modest advance if implemented by ingenious and determined administration by the Department of Justice.[17]

[17] Furthermore, Congress succeeded in passing two carefully limited criminal statutes making it a crime to obstruct court orders by threats of force or to cross a state line in flight from bombing or burning property. In addition, the 1960 statute requires the retention of voting records and provides for action against the state itself in the event that local election officials resign to avoid prosecution. See Ch. IV for a discussion of the enforcement of the new civil rights legislation.

From these two specific legislative instances, the fate of the civil rights proposals in 1957 and 1960, certain general conclusions about presidential legislative initiative seem to flow. Procedural obstacles, mixed legislative priorities, and a reluctance on the part of Congress to move too swiftly in correcting inequality by legislation are barriers to omnibus civil rights legislation which would permit a broad and un-obstructed assertion of Federal protection of Negro rights. It is unlikely that these barriers will fall unless there is a radical alteration of our present legislative pluralism. Presidential leadership, even though it may be more vigorous than the Eisenhower leadership, will be limited accordingly. On the other hand, the political reality of the Negro vote and a growing national conscience about Negro rights present opportunities for presidential leadership which were absent a generation ago. Within the last few years the myth of committee sovereignty over civil rights legislation has been shaken by the fact that the leadership was willing on occasion to bypass committees or to order them to report. Furthermore, the long filibuster over the Civil Rights Act of 1960 was more of a folk drama than a show of force. In sum, although presidential leadership will not bring about swift legislative action in the field of civil rights, the way is now open for piecemeal construction of protective Federal legislation if the President chooses to lead.

Finally, to say that presidential leadership is unlikely to succeed except in piecemeal fashion for many years to come is not to suggest that broad legislative proposals should not come from the White House. Initiative of this kind is not wasted even when there is no prospect that a bill will become law. A generation of filibusters prohibited legislation on lynching, the poll tax, and fair employment practices, but the cumulative publicity of congressional debate was not without its influence. Many Americans in government and out were touched by the facts and rhetoric in the legislative discussion of violence and discrimination.[18] Partly because of congressional consideration over the years, lynching is now a rarity and the poll tax an antiquated method of restricting Negro voting. The debates on a series of fair employment practices bills, including the fact that they failed passage, exposed the problem of discrimination in hiring and intensified the efforts of the Federal executive and state governments to attack what Congress would not. Similarly, had the Civil Rights Acts of 1957 or 1960 died at the last moment in Congress, the very turmoil of debate would have influenced national thinking on the Negro's right to vote. At times, in other words, it may be advisable for the President to initiate civil rights legislation solely for educational effect.

Presidential Leadership against Congress

The President's intervention in the legislative process cannot stop with the proposing of legislation. In fact, as was noted earlier, where First Amendment freedoms or due process of law are involved in legislative proposals, Congress may run away with the bill and make matters worse than before. For this reason and because Congress has a multitude of its own ideas about the Bill of Rights, a President frequently will be forced to exercise defensive techniques if he wishes to counteract legislation or an antilibertarian tone set by the more outspoken elements in Congress.

The White House may attempt to block or modify legislative proposals by means of personal presidential interces-

[18] White, *A Man Called White*, 42, 123.

sion with the leaders in Congress or members of committees formulating policy in the field of constitutional rights. Departmental advice may be given to convince the authors of legislation of the wisdom of less restrictive alternatives, and close co-operation with members of congressional committees will be helpful. There is some evidence that the Truman administration assisted in the preparation of the Tydings committee report on McCarthy's charges of communism in the State Department, for example, and Franklin Roosevelt threw his power into committee consideration of a censorship bill and later in a drastic wire-tap bill by stating his interest in more moderate provisions. The Eisenhower administration, although not without stumbling, opposed outright or sought "further study" of some of the extreme congressional proposals for internal security legislation.[19] The White House must be constantly alert to extreme congressional notions, and the President who wishes to preserve the Bill of Rights must be prepared, in Harry Truman's words, to persuade Congress to "do what they ought to do without persuasion," even though in this field the persuasion most frequently will take the form of persuading Congress not to act. All the traditional weapons of the presidency are available if a President wishes to use them: the patronage, the many small and large gifts which the executive branch

[19] There is scattered but by no means conclusive evidence of administration assistance to the Tydings committee in the Truman Papers, for example, "Suggestions for a Committee Report of the Tydings Subcommittee," May 26, 1950, emanating from the Department of State. For Roosevelt's intervention see F. D. R. to Thomas H. Eliot, Feb. 21, 1941, Franklin D. Roosevelt Papers, Hyde Park, N.Y., and for the somewhat less outspoken opposition of the Eisenhower administration to legislative proposals, *New York Times,* May 1, 1959, June 10, 1959.

can bestow on a member of Congress and his constituency, the countermanding presidential appeal to influential segments of the public through the press and in private correspondence, the veto power, and that which is so frequently forgotten in commentaries on presidential power, appeals to reason itself.

Outspoken presidential disapproval, however it is expressed, offers strength to those who are opposed to restrictive legislation and tends to undermine the certitude of the proponents of statutory patriotism. Whether these weapons will be used when the tide is running against the Bill of Rights will depend on the courage of the President and the depths of his conviction about the Constitution. It is for this reason that the Truman veto of the Internal Security Act has been called one of the notable acts of Harry Truman's political career. The fact that the veto was not sustained by Congress proves that even this last resort of presidential legislative power is ineffectual against hysteria; but the experience suggests other lessons as well. In the first place, the burdens of leadership in the Korean war (and war is always cited as an apology for invasions of constitutional rights) did not prevent the President from dealing with the internal security bill personally or stop him from speaking out against legislation which he believed made "a mockery of the Bill of Rights and of our claims to stand for freedom in the world." [20]

Second, the President introduced into the history of the presidency a principle which others might well follow; that is, according to Harry Truman's view of the office, all legislation should be vetoed which is not in harmony with the

[20] Veto message, *New York Times*, Sept. 23, 1950.

Bill of Rights. In this instance he feared that appeasement in one case would lead to further congressional invasions of individual liberties and establish a pattern of repression throughout the states and localities. The extent of presidential determination to halt the legislation is reflected in his decision to attach an individual note to all members of Congress appealing to them to sustain his veto. "No considerations of expediency," he remarked in his veto message, "can justify the enactment of such a bill as this, a bill which would so weaken our liberties and give aid and comfort to those who would destroy us. I have no alternative but to return this bill without my approval."

And third, the President fulfilled his responsibility to speak out against a destructive congressional mood, an effort which was doomed to failure if measured in practical legislative terms but at the time provided a national voice which declared that there was more than one side to the question. Speaking of the anti-Communist hysteria, the President later remarked, "The office of the presidency is the one office to which all the people turn when they are beset by fears like these. It is to the President that they look to say a firm 'No' to those who wish to destroy others through fear and innuendo." [21] The firm "no" of the presidency, in the language of the veto or otherwise, has been needed in recent years to combat the irresponsible excursions of congressional committees. That the "no" has not always been effective, firm, or determinedly applied is part of the history of the period; but once again difficulties in execution cannot negate the elementary obligation of the President to attempt to

[21] Address at a dinner in honor of President Truman's seventieth birthday, May 8, 1954, *New York Times*, May 9, 1954.

57

check the erosion of constitutional value by all legislative means at his command.

Finally, presidential firmness in dealing with Congress must extend to his own administration. Few would deny that with or without presidential approval the police agencies in the executive branch, in either the interests of administrative convenience or misguided zeal, have pressed for legislation which was neither necessary nor wise. A President is swept up in the conflict between administrative "efficiency," which may call for stringent legislation, and his own obligation to the Bill of Rights. Congressional sympathy will add to the momentum of administrative requests. A President and his White House aides must, therefore, be on guard against departmental parochialism, and the President must be on guard against the prejudices of his White House aides. It is here that the Bureau of the Budget and the White House office play a crucial role for, from this vantage point, the threats to the Bill of Rights in the legislative programs of the departments can be observed and reported directly to the President.[22] He in the end will be the one person in the ad-

[22] The presidential assistants in the Truman White House office were frequently outspoken in their defense of individual liberties. One assistant was styled "our one-man civil liberties union," and correspondence in the Official Files indicates that this spirit was accepted by most of the President's immediate staff. Perhaps when the Eisenhower papers are open for study the same spirit will be evident. Until then, only one individual on the White House staff, Maxwell M. Rabb, truly stands out in the public record in his regard for constitutional guarantees. For an example of alertness against a questionable departmental bill in the Truman White House, one memorandum to the President's counsel is illustrative. It opposed immigration legislation fathered by the Department of Justice which continued the ban against the admission of ex-Communists to the country. After some analysis, the author concluded,

ministration able to snuff out harmful departmental proposals. And because the origins of so-called "legislative" violations of constitutional liberty are found frequently within the walls of the executive departments it is imperative, if the President is to maintain guard over the Bill of Rights, that such legislative proposals become "administration," not "departmental," measures when and if they get to Congress. There is little wisdom in permitting the Post Office Department or the Department of Justice to deal directly with Congress in requesting restrictive legislation without having the proposals and supporting testimony pass in detail through the more disinterested filter of presidential attention. On the other hand, and this more than once was the experience in the Eisenhower administration, it is self-defeating if a department opposes restrictive legislation without the concerted and vocal backing of the White House.

The White House will always find it difficult to combat the natural alliance between the police agencies of the administration and security-minded members of Congress. But it is possible for the President to oppose these natural affinities by making his wishes specifically and completely clear. In this regard, a letter from President Truman to his Attorney General concerning internal security legislation might be titled a Model Statement of Presidential Intent:

In summary, this is my thinking on the matter. Our internal security laws must be adequate. To the extent that they are not adequate now, they should be strengthened. Excessive security, however, can be as dangerous as inadequate security. Excessive

---

"All that is really at stake is the Justice Department's administrative comfort—which is hardly a sufficient basis for national policy" (David E. Bell to Charles Murphy, March 12, 1951, Truman Papers).

59

security brings normal administrative operations to a standstill, prevents the interchange of ideas necessary to scientific progress, and—most important of all—encroaches on the individual rights and freedoms which distinguish a democracy from a totalitarian country.

Every proposal for new internal security laws, therefore, should be carefully scrutinized not only from the standpoint of how much it will add to national security but also from the standpoint of the other considerations noted above, and particularly the last.[23]

The Presidents and Senator McCarthy

To some extent Presidents will always be called upon to offset those attacks on the Bill of Rights which originate in political ambition and smallness of mind in Congress. On occasion a political figure or political movement will appear and spread doubts about the constitutional tradition to the nation at large. Both the Eisenhower and Truman administrations experienced two and a half years of this type of anticonstitutionalism in Senator McCarthy's crusade against "Communists in Government." In the early days of McCarthyism the Truman administration limited its opposition to co-operation with the Tydings subcommittee (investigating alleged subversion in the Department of State) and a series of denials of McCarthy's charges. At first the President seemed to follow the strategy of silence which his successor was to adopt in an effort to deny free publicity to the Senator. As McCarthy's power grew, however, so did the

[23] Harry S. Truman to Attorney General McGrath, May 19, 1950, Truman Papers. And see the President's press conference, Aug. 19, 1948, in the same collection.

President's aggressiveness. In press conference the President spoke of the Senator as the Kremlin's greatest asset and on one occasion "the pathological McCarthy." [24] In his public addresses, furthermore, he spoke against hysteria and on one notable occasion carried his attack to some of the Senator's spiritual brethren when he addressed the American Legion. It was a significant reaffirmation of the Bill of Rights at a time when few in public life were willing to speak out. Attacking those who were "chipping away our basic freedoms" by broadcasting suspicion and unproved charges, the President with a touch of irony congratulated the Legion on its 100 per cent Americanism:

Real Americanism means that we will protect freedom of speech —we will defend the right of people to say what they think, regardless of how much we may disagree with them.

Real Americanism means freedom of religion. It means that we will not discriminate against a man because of his religious faith.

Real Americanism means fair opportunities for all our citizens. It means that none of our citizens shall be held back by unfair discrimination and prejudice.

Real Americanism means fair play. It means that a man who is accused of a crime shall be considered innocent until he has been proved guilty. It means that people are not to be penalized and persecuted for exercising their Constitutional liberties.

Real Americanism means also that liberty is not license. There is no freedom to injure others. The Constitution does not protect free speech to the extent of permitting conspiracies to overthrow the Government. Neither does the right of free speech authorize slander or character assassination. These limitations are essential to keep us working together in one great community.

[24] The President's press conference, Jan. 31, 1952, Truman Papers.

Real Americanism includes all these things. And it takes all of them together to make 100 per cent Americanism—the kind the Legion is pledged to support.[25]

This unadorned restatement of the constitutional values then under attack was a presidential warning without immediate effect, but it tended to counteract the dominant congressional and public tone of hostility and indifference to constitutional guarantees. The President was hamstrung by the effects of postwar disillusion and the current frustration of the Korean war-without-victory. His words seemed to carry less weight, too, owing to the heritage of Democratic naïveté about communism during World War II and his own unfortunate "red-herring" description of the Hiss investigation.[26] He was, above all, a Democrat serving his last two years in office. The unenviable task of counteracting McCarthy's energy and congressional complacency became a Republican responsibility. What, in the end, came to distinguish the Eisenhower and Truman strategies was not that one or the other "stopped" McCarthy, for neither did. Rather, the distinguishing feature was that in one case the President spoke out unequivocally for the Bill of Rights and defended members of his administration from attack while the other President finally accepted a strategy of virtual silence and compromise.

How effective President Eisenhower's strategy was will be a source of debate for some years to come. The Republican

[25] Address at the dedication of the Washington headquarters of the American Legion, Aug. 14, 1951, *New York Times,* Aug. 15, 1951.

[26] On this point see the excellent discussion in Harold W. Chase, *Security and Liberty: The Problem of Native Communists, 1947–1955* (New York, 1955), 77–79.

President's dilemma was rooted in Senator McCarthy's attachment to a wing of the President's own party together with the President's personal aversion to controversy and his theory that presidential power should be restrained in those areas in which Congress was, or ought to be, dominant. Like Truman, moreover, Eisenhower hesitated to confer presidential publicity on the Senator's cause by engaging in an open contest. The pattern of stern public aloofness, once the nominee became President, could not hide his personal disapproval of McCarthy's methods. "In private," the best authority on the inner workings of the administration in this period remarks, "he could go up in an utter blaze over him. McCarthy's tactics disgusted and infuriated him." [27] In the early stages of the Senator's dealings with the new administration the President, hoping that public opinion would control the investigator, withdrew from any public criticism of the Senator. As the tempo of McCarthy's activities increased and his aims became more apparent, a struggle began within the White House over the choice of tactics. Some urged patience and silence on the give-him-enough-rope theory. Others wanted the President to provide tree, rope, and a public bill of particulars. Ultimately, neither group prevailed and a firm strategy was never determined. Instead, as Robert J. Donovan writes:

Most, although not all, of those who were closest to this problem in the White House do not believe that the President followed any carefully planned, deliberate strategy toward McCarthy. In their opinion it was an attitude rather than a strategy that guided him.

[27] Robert J. Donovan, *Eisenhower: The Inside Story* (New York, 1956), 247.

If there is any single word that can epitomize this attitude, it is disdain.[28]

Disdain, coupled with the Eisenhower doctrine of presidential self-restraint, established a pattern which by default favored the enough-rope theory, even though the pattern was broken by presidential intervention on several occasions. Most of these interventions occurred when the President's powers in foreign affairs were challenged, for example, in the Bohlen nomination, East-West trade with Communist China, and the President's directive during the Army-McCarthy hearings in 1954 prohibiting the release to Congress of confidential exchanges between members of the executive branch. Where the climate of liberty was threatened more directly, the President was not as active. He did speak out in opposition to the article by J. B. Matthews in the *American Mercury* accusing great numbers of the Protestant clergy of Communist sympathies and thereby contributed to the dismissal of Matthews from McCarthy's staff. In the midst of the Senator's investigation of the Voice of America and the International Information Administration the President warned against book burning; he averted a McCarthy investigation of the Central Intelligence Agency and attempted to have the Army-McCarthy hearings transferred from the Committee on Government Operations to the more judicious Armed Services Committee.[29] But the record of the time shows more instances of hesitancy than outspoken opposition. As for the Secretary of State and other presidential advisers, the McCarthy attack quickly overran the threshold of resistance.

The surrender of the Department of State to Senator Mc-

[28] *Ibid.*, 257.   [29] *Ibid.*, 225.

Carthy's attacks is well known. Individual administrators such as Theodore Kaghan, acting deputy director for the Public Affairs Division of the High Commissioner's office in Germany, and Reed Harris, deputy administrator of the International Information Administration, were sacrificed to the fantasies of the investigator's memory of earlier ideological indiscretions. The retirement of these men and others led to a decrease in administrative efficiency, while the effectiveness of the information program was weakened further by a series of urgent directives attempting to define what "left-wing" writings could be placed on the Information Administration's shelves abroad. The directives accomplished nothing but to show the world the extent to which the Department of State was "confused, worried, and anxious to appease." [30] If one restricts judgment to the barest limits of constitutionalism, sound foreign policy, or administrative efficiency, this characteristic administrative response to McCarthyism remains unjustified. The administration's attack on its agency and the appointment of Scott McLeod to the individually tailored post of personnel and security officer in the Department of State lacked even the refined subtlety of political maneuver. So, too, did the presence of Senator McCarthy at the White House the day the administration announced the newly formulated personnel security program in 1953. What the administration took to be necessary concessions to gain a Senator's co-operation became, in fact, to opponents, supporters, and the indifferent, symbolic acts of submission or approval.

[30] Robert E. Cushman, *Civil Liberties in the United States* (Ithaca, 1956), 46; Martin Merson, *The Private Diary of a Public Servant* (New York, 1955).

It is impossible to judge the depth of the President's personal involvement in the formulation of these concessions. One notes the occasional glimmer of presidential indignation shining through a curtain of misguided political maneuvering. In general, however, the uncertain and dismaying twists of policy were evidence of a fundamental miscalculation. To believe that McCarthy could be silenced by concessions—however damaging to individual liberties—or that he would accept a doctrine of live and let live was to underestimate the force of his following and his fascination with his own demagoguery. The fact remains that the theory of enough-rope merely raised the question of how the Senator would use it. In the brief time the rope was in his hands, as knout or noose, serious damage was done to American foreign policy, to the civil service, and most certainly to constitutional liberty. Whether the President and the Secretary of State by speaking out in a vigorous and sustained manner would have prevailed over the political force and popularity of McCarthy's cause without Senate action cannot now be decided. The question is, in fact, not at issue, for constitutional morality, like all other, is not measured by the degree of its immediate success. That the President and his advisers miscalculated is undeniable; undeniable too is the bankruptcy of constitutional sensibility on the part of many members of the administration. The constitutional obligation was clearly to attempt to work the ingredients of the Secretary of State's loyal churchmanship into the workaday threats to the sanctity of the individual and to apply the tough individualism of the best of the Republican party tradition against the temptations of administrative convenience.

If we accept, as we must, that presidential words are acts

and acts take on symbolic meaning, the President was poorly advised in his policy of silence and periodic concessions. President Eisenhower, at the height of his popularity in these years, was the "one man in the country able to match his prestige against McCarthy with confidence as to the results." [31] The attainable result in this instance was not the end of the Senator's political career or even an end to his attacks on the administration. Rather the President had the opportunity to bolster the voices of opposition to McCarthyism within his own administration, in Congress, and in the press by attaching to their protest the prestige of the presidency. Instead, during this period certain essential constitutional values found no sustained national representation. In sum, for all of the President's personal indignation, the Eisenhower example is a case study in what the executive branch should not do if the intention is to counteract a hostile congressional tone toward individual liberty. The Senate eventually censured McCarthy for action which brought the Senate into disrepute, but not because of his running attack on the Constitution. Silence can be used to accomplish a presidential purpose, although not the defense of liberties under this type of attack. There was a void in this case which the President, it seems, was constitutionally obliged to fill.

Presidential Silence

Among the infinite shadings of effective legislative strategy in the interest of constitutional rights, silence does not always herald the bankruptcy of presidential leadership. Silence, as an expression of presidential indifference, may be sufficient

[31] Richard H. Rovere, *The Eisenhower Years* (New York, 1956), 188.

to defeat a proposal originating in Congress. Such silence may be a device to avoid stimulating public reaction which, in turn, might stiffen congressional resolve to act. Further, the executive branch may act alone, hoping that administrative efforts may escape the hornet's nest of congressional opposition. Clearly this reasoning was partially responsible for the two major executive orders dealing with the loyalty-security programs under the Truman and Eisenhower administrations. There is little doubt that the Presidents were attempting to inaugurate satisfactory programs and thus forestall more extreme congressional measures.

Presidents have bargained for congressional silence more effectively in the field of minority rights, although, because of the nature of such agreements, the available evidence is only circumstantial.[32] A President in such cases may trade the loss of favorable publicity for congressional silence, accomplishing the program without arousing the South to intense criticism of its representatives in Congress. The reputed agreement between President Truman and Congress in which forceful legislative leadership for civil rights was traded for congressional acquiescence in administrative measures to extend fair employment and desegregation in the armed forces cannot be documented and, one suspects, will remain one of the minor loose ends of history. Much the

[32] The Truman Papers contain some evidence of the administration's interest in keeping some civil rights questions out of Congress. One memorandum was written to discourage congressional attention to discrimination in housing. "We are making progress in the practice of non-discrimination in the field of housing as we are in other fields, by the use of administrative measures, far more rapidly than we will if we engage in legislative battles which arise when hard and fast clauses are introduced on the Hill" (Philleo Nash to Charles S. Murphy, Sept. 20, 1951).

same can be said of similar advances under the Eisenhower administration.

What is clear, however, is that the chief executive's natural inclination to celebrate administrative advances in civil rights may bring about Southern countermeasures as constituency pressures mount. Silence, then, may be politically damaging but administratively advantageous. It is difficult to prove but interesting to contemplate the assertion that desegregation in the armed forces was accomplished in this manner. According to one scholar:

Both Southern and Northern congressmen entered the conspiracy of silence, so that the full import of the new policy did not become generally known until the end of 1953. By that time desegregation was virtually a *fait accompli* throughout all branches of the armed service, and there was no turning back.

An army officer spoke in the same vein:

We agreed there would be no publicity. We were afraid that if there were a lot of stories in the papers, southern congressmen would have to get up on their hind legs and oppose it. We wanted to get it done without fanfare—then tell about it.[33]

[33] C. Vann Woodward, *The Strange Career of Jim Crow* (New York, 1957), 136; Lee Nichols, *Breakthrough on the Color Front* (New York, 1954), 134 and ch. xv, generally. That it may be to the advantage of minority groups to avoid the legislative "kiss of death" is evident in Representative William L. Dawson's testimony on civil rights legislation in 1959. Dawson opposed the establishment by Congress of a Commission on Equal Job Opportunity partly because the President had already established a committee by executive order. "It seems to me," Mr. Dawson testified, "that this proposal would simply subject the President's Committee to the hazards of political controversy and the threat of future slicing of appropriations, and would be only a kiss of death to an existing program" (*Hearings before a Subcommittee*

President Eisenhower limited to a minimum his announcements about desegregation in the District of Columbia and Federal establishments. After the Supreme Court segregation decision in 1954, he made a single statement to the effect that he would make the District of Columbia the show place of the nation. Thereafter, the White House moved quietly under the direction of Maxwell M. Rabb to wipe out governmentally authorized segregation in the nation's capital and extend it to other Federal institutions throughout the country. Although the President's silence served liberty poorly during the McCarthy episode, the conscious policy of silence served it well in another. One of the greatest accomplishments of the Eisenhower administration in the field of civil rights was effected without the political advantages of clamorous publicity. The difficult decision to be made in these matters, consequently, is the complex one of whether silence or vigorous executive maneuvering in Congress or a dramatic public stand will best serve the interests of constitutional rights.

Conclusion

Needless to say, the varieties of presidential maneuver discussed above can, and have been used to, damage rather than protect individual liberties. Silence may be a sign of White House indifference or insensitivity. Presidents may intensify the antilibertarian tone in Congress, as did President Eisenhower when he proposed in his State of the Union message in 1954 an act withdrawing citizenship from those convicted

of the [House] Committee on the Judiciary, 86th Cong., 1st Sess., pp. 177–178 [1959]).

under the Smith Act. A President's legislative proposals have all too frequently sought to impair individual liberty. Such was the case when Harry Truman asked for authority to draft strikers into the Army and when the Eisenhower administration initiated programs in Congress to extend wire-tapping and passport legislation. On more than a few occasions, in an unbalanced search for security legislation, the executive branch has played into the hands of the elements in Congress least friendly to constitutional restraints, while agency heads have resisted legislation reducing their own discretion to cut into the substance of liberty.

Presidential maneuver in the interest of constitutional rights, consequently, is properly enlivened only when the White House accepts the protection of liberty as a major responsibility. It presupposes a presidency energetic in legislative combat and a President with a staff which considers the immediate and long-run interests of liberty as a primary calculation in all policy making. It assumes, too, that the President will keep a jealous eye on the legislative alliances of his police agencies and that, by making all legislation affecting civil liberties a question of concern at the highest level, he will assure that they pass through the formidable barrier of his own presumption against their existence as law.

But even when the President confronts the problem of legislative leadership, he has only begun to meet his responsibility. For whether congressional statutes are restrictive and passed for real or fancied reasons of security or to guarantee civil rights, or whether the law issues from the decisions of the Federal courts, the President must administer them. Prudent administration, whatever the legislative foun-

71

dations, can spell the difference between the survival of constitutional rights and a new bureaucratic tyranny. Important as legislative maneuver may be, execution and administration remain the most vital portion of the President's responsibility.

III

Administrative Affirmation
and Restraint

MOST Americans are aware of the broad impact which presidential conduct has on national security, prosperity, or other aspects of the public welfare. They involve the hard and immediate facts of survival and material comfort. But few perceive clearly what is ultimately of equal value, the consequences of administrative policy and practice for constitutional liberty. Similarly, few are aware of the great measure of administrative power which is on hand to enable the President and his subordinates to act positively to protect and extend individual liberties. Authority to assist or damage liberty is found in the Constitution, the statutes, and the decisions of administrators and judges. All are enlivened by continual administrative interpretation. Whatever conditions the law may impose, the spirit with which the law is administered will have a profound effect on the durability of the nation's system of constitutional rights.

The scope of the chief executive's responsibility is found in the character of presidential power and the experience of the current administrative generation. Although in broad terms it embraces the administrative qualities of affirmation and restraint, the immediate responsibility at this point in our history is to revitalize the liberty shaken by the nation's adjustment to the Cold War and, at the same time, to apply the energy of the executive branch to the amelioration of the painful social crisis over the Negro question. The President, in a word, may attempt to control the excesses in his own house while broadening the sphere of liberty by positive administrative action and the just execution of the laws. We ask much of our Presidents, in this field of public policy no less than others; and, as elsewhere, the encumbrances on affirmative action are plentiful. The purpose of this chapter and the next is to describe these encumbrances, the errors of a generation, or more, and the instruments available to the President as he attempts to overcome both.

The Administrative Environment

It should be emphasized at the outset that the executive attitude toward minorities in the 1940's and 1950's differed widely from the attitudes toward First Amendment freedoms and due process of law. As for the latter, despite steady criticism from without and doubts and protests within the government, the administrative record was predominantly dismal and marked by a doubling and redoubling of encroachments on individual liberty. One need only note the successive flowering of increasingly severe security tests for employment in the Federal government which are characteristic of misapplied administrative discretion. As Dean Acheson has pointed out in a notable *mea culpa*, "What was, at first, designed for cases which it was thought would be serious, sensitive, and rare, became commonplace and routine." [1] The Federal employee security program, once limited to only the most sensitive positions and with the burden of proof on the government, swept the entire executive branch of the national government and spread presumptively to state and local governments as well as private industry. The rights of privacy, association, and conscience suffered under the redoubled momentum of successive tests. The original Truman program required the government to establish *reasonable grounds* for belief in the disloyalty of the government employee; in 1951 the burden shifted to the employee when the test became the administration's *reasonable doubts* as to the loyalty of the employee; and in 1953 an even more stringent test permitted employment only if *clearly consistent* with national security.[2] Executive orders were bolstered by statutory authority, and reform was hampered by the administrative and congressional mood. By and large the executive needed little congressional encouragement for its own policies. The trend of these tests in loyalty security is strikingly parallel to a generation of mounting restrictions in passport policy, government secrecy, and post-office censorship.

The treatment of the civil rights of minorities is in marked contrast. Here a more salutary trend of executive action developed (although not without serious shortcomings in vis-

[1] *A Democrat Looks at His Party* (New York, 1955), 129.

[2] The now-famous Executive Orders are 9835, 10241, and 10450. See Ralph S. Brown, *Loyalty and Security* (New Haven, 1958), 31, 50. That the executive branch attempted to take quiet advantage of *Cole* v. *Young,* 351 U.S. 536 (1956), *Vitarelli* v. *Seaton,* 359 U.S. 535 (1959), and *Greene* v. *McElroy,* 360 U.S. 474 (1959), which had the effect of limiting the program to "sensitive" positions and imposed other limitations on the loyalty-security program was one of several hopeful signs that a more sensible trend was emerging.

ion and execution) largely because political interest more frequently coincided with administrative inclination. The influential report of the Truman Committee on Civil Rights, the inroads made into discrimination in private and public employment, not to mention desegregation in the armed forces or the severe extension of executive power in Little Rock, all mark a decisive shift in executive policy. Consequently, the future problem for the executive in dealing with minority problems is to bring a greater measure of wise planning and wholehearted determination to bear on an already praiseworthy predisposition.

The struggle here is against excessive administrative caution and prejudice within the government. The problem is not, as with First Amendment and procedural protections, one of reintroducing restraint but rather of overcoming an inclination toward timidity induced by the power of the South in Congress and lack of any over-all programmatic direction. Despite the great advances in the last decade, the executive has failed to use the available weapons with persistent vigor. As a result, the need in the area of minority rights is to enliven further an already constructive trend; and for the traditional restraints of the Bill of Rights, the problem is one of creating a new mood and an adjustment to Cold War pressures. In both instances, the President's duty is to hasten and guide his administration while profiting by candid reflection on past errors.

The barriers to presidential leadership are formidable. Short of a libertarian's Utopia, moreover, they will never be fully overcome. Beyond the obstructions of federalism and the separation of powers are certain institutional realities and a cluster of newly intensified administrative presuppositions. Unfortunately, the same forces which create the problem complicate the solution. The impersonality of modern bureaucracy, for example, invites violations of individual liberty, while the size which contributes to the impersonality makes presidential control more difficult. Or it may be in the best interest of a sound foreign policy to protect liberty at home, but the encroaching demands of security—related equally to a sound foreign policy—will not rest. There is no easy escape from these paradoxes.

The foremost barrier is that the presidential office today is attuned primarily to foreign affairs. The interests of national security absorb the President's time and energy while, at the same time, national security determines his priorities. All else, if the first impulse alone is considered, may be swept up in this prime responsibility. Even though, in the end, security may best be preserved within a system where ideas and speech flow freely or where equal rights are protected, it takes considerable courage and vision to risk the felt necessities of immediate security for the seemingly abstract and intangible benefits of freedom. The task is complicated further because the President can never choose *between* liberty and security but must find somewhere along the wavering line separating the two that point where each will be best served. Throughout history, unless under conditions of despotism or anarchy, the solution has never been automatic. Harold Stassen, in testimony before a congressional committee, spoke of the dilemma as it appeared in the loyalty security program. Deciding whether a government employee is a security risk is, he commented,

the most complex problem in the world. It is the most difficult decision to make. You have on the one hand the tremendous tragic

77

damage that can be done to your country if you have a security risk in a responsible sensitive position in the Government.

On the other hand, you have a deep, penetrating personal injury that can occur if you wrongly label a man. Here you sit in the Government and you must balance these two without any situation which turns up red and green like a stop and go signal.

Or, as one White House aide has remarked of his own experience with the loyalty-security program, "There were not many things over there [in the White House] that tortured me, but this was one of them." [3]

For the President, who has ultimate administrative responsibility for the character of such programs, the task is made no easier when administrative time and energy are of necessity burned up in his responsibility for national survival. Much the same pressures confront his subordinates.

An equally important obstacle to White House guardianship of liberty is the growth of the bureaucracy and its contemporary character. Under the pressures of the Cold War and the natural tendency of all bureaus to magnify their own importance, administrative discretion is abused and the "inefficiencies" of due process are circumvented. Parkinson's law of accumulating manpower carries with it in this case a corollary of accumulating legalism which serves to shield an agency from the embarrassment of thought or imaginative use of discretion. The growth tends, too, to divorce the President and his immediate staff from working knowledge of the real activities of the agencies and effective

---

[3] *Hearings before a Subcommittee of the (Senate) Committee on Post Office and Civil Service*, 84th Cong., 1st and 2d Sess., p. 715 (hereinafter cited as Johnston Committee); interview with Mr. Charles S. Murphy, April 15, 1958.

control. Because congressional laurels have been bestowed on those administrators who have shown zeal for security, the agencies have exaggerated the importance and purity of their own functions, knowing full well that they will need the help of Congress long after the President and his senior administrators return to private life. And so the loyalty-security operation, the passport program, the deportation of aliens, post-office censorship, and others have tended to become islands of policy and power frequently removed from direct presidential control. Once given a President's determination to introduce respect for individual rights as an important element in administrative policy making, methods exist for overcoming the distance between presidential purpose and agency insularity; but all are conditioned by the same administrative realities which create the distance in the first place. What Clinton Rossiter calls administrative "pluralism," [4] or the fundamental loyalty of each agency to itself, is compounded by clashing administrative interests or personal ambition, the special influence of congressional committees and extragovernmental pressure groups, or the honest urge of the agency to get its job done. In view of these factors, respect for constitutional rights, without the presidential presence, may appear far down the list of agency priorities. There will be a tendency to avoid disrupting old administrative patterns, whether embracing racial discrimination or not, and a tendency to avoid introducing "extraneous" factors, such as the observance of due process of law, which may reduce administrative "efficiency." Statements may be made which reflect a formal

[4] Clinton Rossiter, *The American Presidency* (New York, 1960), 59–61.

attachment to nondiscrimination or due process of law, but the real practices may diverge from the stated policy.

Furthermore, because in-fighting is a part of the natural condition of administration, political and personal ambition will shape administrative purpose, agency may conflict with agency, and personality will conflict with personality. Even a partial list of administrative experiences with constitutional rights over the last few years will illustrate this: the struggle between (and within) the Department of Justice and the Army over the removal of Japanese-Americans from the West Coast in 1942; the resistance met by some members of the White House staff in the Truman administration to their efforts to reduce discrimination by Federal agencies or the conflict with the White House and within the Department of Justice over the need for additional internal security legislation; the apparent untouchability of the Passport Office of the Department of State and the Immigration and Naturalization Service in the same period; the reputed conflicts among members of President Eisenhower's Committee on Government Contracts and between some members and the Secretary of Labor; or the differences in attitude between some members of the White House staff and some officials of the Department of Justice over the type of civil rights legislation to initiate in 1960. All are ordinary examples of the divisive effect of conflicting interests and administrative politics. Administrative pluralism underlies the continuing challenge to the President's leadership and control; while creating the need for presidential oversight, it also hinders its operation.

Administrative Patterns

"The risks of all government regulations," one commentator has written, "particularly where applicable to great numbers of cases, [are] the inexorable drift to routine, ultracautious standards and the reliance on narrow, frightened minor officials."[5] The pattern imposed by size and administrative pluralism is itself a considerable obstruction to corrective measures originating in the White House. Equally important, however, is a cluster of deeply ingrained attitudes peculiar to the Cold War period which have tended to overrun due process of law and the responsible use of administrative discretion. In order to counteract these attitudes it is necessary to struggle against the administrative ideology of a generation.

These attitudes have encouraged the abuse of discretion and embedded in the administrative mind a presumption of validity for restrictive acts on the part of the executive branch. Representatives of this spirit are found in all agencies, but particularly those dealing directly with national security—Defense, State, Justice—and such bureaus as Immigration and Naturalization, the Passport Office, the National Security Council, and the FBI. The essence of these administrative presuppositions is best summed up in the term "cop mentality" or, euphemistically, the professionalization of security personnel. The appearance of that new American type, the security officer, is a symbol of the change, as is the important and elementary valuation given to the needs of "the [military] managers of violence" in high

[5] Louis L. Jaffe, "The Right to Travel: The Passport Problem," *Foreign Affairs*, 35: 27 (Oct., 1956).

policy councils.[6] The impulse to security is strengthened by following the age-old administrative maxim that the best way to accomplish your goal and to increase your agencies' appropriations is to magnify the need for its services.

Unfortunately, this type of professional zeal moves beyond the bounds of security to other fields of control. Thus, the same spirit pervades post-office censorship of literature, while government information is labeled secret to protect the administrator from criticism, and passports are denied on grounds far distant from the needs of national security. The police mentality assumes its own virtue. In the name of security or morality controls are placed on persons or information in a quest for symmetry of national belief and action. The instrument of this virtue is the abundant use of administrative discretion and, frequently, the twisting of statutory authorization.

The process is evident in the evolving powers of proscription in several Federal agencies. The Post Office Department over the years has constructed an edifice of censorship on the shakiest of statutory authority.[7] This agency gathered to itself power to revoke second-class mailing privileges

[6] This is Harold Lasswell's term. See Samuel P. Huntington, *The Soldier and the State* (Cambridge, 1947), 11. Robert E. Cushman puts it succinctly when he speaks of military men "in whom a zeal for secrecy is an occupational disease" ("Freedom vs. Security," *Physics Today*, 2: 16 [March, 1949]).

[7] J. C. N. Paul and M. L. Schwartz, "Obscenity in the Mails: A Comment on Some Problems of Federal Censorship," *University of Pennsylvania Law Review*, 106: 214–253 (Dec., 1957); Edward De Grazia, "Obscenity and the Mail: A Study of Administrative Restraint," *Law and Contemporary Problems*, 20: 608–620 (Autumn, 1955); Walter Gellhorn, *Individual Freedom and Governmental Restraints* (Baton Rouge, 1956), 83–104.

of numerous magazines, including that American staple, *Esquire*,[8] and without benefit of formal appeal used a mail-block sanction (prohibiting the delivery of all mail to offending sources of "obscene" publications and other articles), while it declared nondeliverable such volumes as James Jones's *From Here to Eternity*, Alberto Moravia's *Woman of Rome*, and the works of John O'Hara, John Steinbeck, Richard Wright, Ernest Hemingway, and Simone de Beauvoir.[9] It is a challenging task, even for those who are qualified, to define "obscenity." It is obvious in these cases, as it was when Postmaster Summerfield found *Lady Chatterley's Lover* obscene, that administrative capacity fell far wide of the mark.

The Post Office Department should be condemned for its literary ignorance, although it may claim some latitude of error in its attempt to check the profitable trade in pornography. There is no excuse, on the other hand, for the discretion which, in company with the Bureau of Customs, it has manufactured for the crude censorship of "foreign propaganda." By means of a tortured interpretation of the Foreign Agents Registration Act of 1938, first by Attorney General Jackson in 1940 and extended subsequently by the Post Office itself, material from beyond the seas and from either

---

[8] *Hannegan* v. *Esquire*, 327 U.S. 146 (1946).

[9] De Grazia, "Obscenity and the Mail," 613–617. Indirect administrative coercion was suggested in the banning of *Lady Chatterley's Lover* when it was reliably reported that an informal warning was given to the *New Yorker;* if it accepted book-club advertising for the volume, it was said, the magazine might not be accepted for mailing (*Washington Post and Times Herald*, May 8, 1959). Under a law passed by Congress in 1960, the mail-block sanction may not be used without an order from a Federal court (*New York Times*, July 4, 1960).

83

side of the Iron Curtain may be seized and destroyed unless the recipient—frequently ignorant of the action of the Post Office Department or the Bureau of Customs—justifies the legitimacy of his own use of the materials. The Solicitor of the Post Office Department gave an authoritative statement of administrative presumption of validity for this type of executive restriction on individual liberty when he promised that "no qualified recipients will be denied these publications. All they have to do is *satisfy us* that they have a legitimate reason for reading them." [10]

Many strange fish have been caught in this net. Lenin's *Selected Works, The Happy Life of Children in the Rumanian People's Republic,* and the London *Economist* have all become entangled in the misuse of discretion. In 1954 an unfriendly study of the Roman Catholic Church was declared to be foreign propaganda and unmailable, as one authority stated "because, presumably, it might 'promote racial, religious, or social dissensions.'" And in one of the most remarkable cases of administrative self-righteousness, the Post Office Department delayed a shipment of seventy-five copies of Lenin's *State and Revolution* for use in a history course at Brown University until the university authorities had explained "the nature of its utility to the University and the restrictions placed on its accessibility." [11]

[10] Dorothy Kahn, "Abe Goff, Our Chief Censor," *Reporter*, May 19, 1955, p. 27.

[11] Gellhorn, *Individual Freedom and Governmental Restraints,* 86 and *passim;* "Government Exclusion of Foreign Political Propaganda," *Harvard Law Review,* 68: 1393–1409 (June, 1955); M. L. Schwartz and J. C. N. Paul, "Foreign Communist Propaganda in the Mails," *University of Pennsylvania Law Review,* 107: 621–666, 796–801 (March, April, 1959).

One doubts that these seventy-five volumes would have turned Providence into another Kronstadt. The sometimes bothersome and modest right to do one's own "discarding into wastebaskets" [12] as well as a rich source of information has been restricted by the Post Office Department's sense of its own virtue and the consequent use of generous administrative discretion.

A somewhat similar administrative presumption by the Passport Office was cast in doubt by the Supreme Court in 1958. The experience before the Supreme Court acted is nonetheless instructive. The Department of State manufactured wide discretion by means of ever-expanding administrative readings of original statutory and constitutional authority.

The tale is an uncommonly instructive and suggestive one. It features the subtle transformation of an instrument invented to aid and protect the traveller—the passport—into a means of control and restriction. It features also a consistent evasion of legislative responsibility, manifested by vacuous mandates to administrative officers; and, in consequence, it exemplifies administrative negativism, timidity, even denseness and caprice, and of course sensitivity to the irresponsible pressure of this or that Congressional panjandrum.[13]

[12] Gellhorn, *Individual Freedom and Governmental Restraints*, 87. "They should not be forced to declare in advance that they have 'a legitimate reason' (or, indeed, any reason at all) for either reading or ignoring books, pamphlets, magazines, newspapers, or circulars. Whether a person reads or burns a publication is his business, not the government's" (*ibid.*, 87–88).

[13] Alexander M. Bickel, "Congressional Review of Passport Policy," *New Republic*, Dec. 29, 1958, pp. 9–10. See *Kent v. Dulles*, 357 U.S. 116 (1958).

Acts of Congress going back to 1856 permit the Secretary of State to issue passports, and a series of executive orders and departmental regulations outline the procedure and standards in time of peace and emergency. But nowhere is specific statutory authority found enabling the Secretary of State to prohibit travel when it is against "the best interests of the United States." The source of this broad prohibition is the President's inherent power to conduct foreign relations and a broad departmental reading of the statute. After 1951 Secretaries Acheson and Dulles applied departmental restrictions with more severity and increased rigidity. The myopic application of discretion was used to prohibit scientists, including Nobel prize winner Linus Pauling, from going abroad (until the announcement of the prize), and others who carried with them no more than a suspicion of slightly tinged, but hardly lethal, reputations for political dissent. Under his power to limit passports to prescribed geographical areas Secretary Dulles refused to permit newsmen to study at firsthand Far Eastern inscrutability, on the grounds that, though there is a constitutional right to publish the news, there is no constitutional right to travel to Communist China to gather it. The pyramid of restrictive power rested on self-appointed administrative discretion.

There are many other examples of this type of administrative imperialism. Wire tapping is one of them. By means of twisted statutory construction, and admittedly with good reason in some instances, the Federal government engages in the activity. Wire tapping is in clear defiance of the literal wording of the Communications Act of 1934 ("No person not being authorized by the sender shall intercept any communication and divulge or publish the existence, contents, substance, purport, effect, or meaning of such intercepted communication"), but the Department of Justice reasons that intercepting *and* divulging, not interception alone, are prohibited by the statute.[14] In another instance, the Department of the Army used doubtful statutory authority to decide unilaterally that the power to award discharges included the power to award less than honorable discharges to inductees with flawless army records but with a history of tainted preinduction associations and activities.[15] Government secrecy policy, in turn, has relied to a large extent on the generous interpretation of the government's "housekeeping" statute and an assortment of executive and departmental orders.[16]

The police mentality, a presumption of validity for restrictive measures, the uninhibited use of administrative discretion, and the impatience with due process of law so evident in the above examples are all incorporated in the post-World War II administrative pattern as it affects civil liberty. But the pattern has been burned even more deeply by other presuppositions and styles of administrative behavior.

For one thing, the administrator has tended to dehumanize the recipients of his disfavor. The confused and sometimes ruthless drive for 100 per cent security has carried with it, all too frequently, what John P. Roche has aptly called "the

[14] Samuel Dash *et al.*, *The Eavesdroppers* (New Brunswick, N.J., 1959), 31, 393–394; Alan Westin, "Wiretapping: The Quiet Revolution," *Commentary*, 29: 338 (April, 1960).

[15] This policy was repudiated by government counsel and overturned in *Harmon* v. *Brucker*, 355 U.S. 579 (1958).

[16] For comments on government secrecy policy see Ch. V.

withering of decency." [17] As a consequence, the day to day administration of government programs is blemished by a more than occasional heartlessness devoid of courage and by an appalling absence of the vital constitutional sense of what should "just not be done." Many of the shortcomings of government security programs are traceable to the failure to appreciate the moderating influence of common-sense decisions and to recognize the warm-blooded nature of the individual caught up in the regulations. Many individuals were discharged under the Federal employee security programs for alleged and real activities and associations in the past which were devoid of significance for later suitability. Unreasonable delay while arriving at decisions concerning the security status of individuals was compounded by the flimsy and suspect nature of the original charges. As a past Solicitor General has commented:

There has been a tendency, because of inexperience and because of pressure from those seeking political advantage, to place undue emphasis upon trivial incidents and circumstances, and to build up theories of guilt by association—theories under which nets could be woven of sufficient width to entrap almost everybody.[18]

Unnecessary suspension on minor charges reflected a striking indifference in many cases to the financial or personal plight of the "accused." The abuse of the authority to suspend suspect individuals from employment while their security or loyalty status was determined is attested to in the conclusions of one writer:

[17] John P. Roche, "A Sane View of Non-conformity," *New Republic*, Feb. 6, 1956, p. 14.

[18] Philip B. Perlman, *Hearings* before the Johnston Committee, 110.

A standard technique was developed by which, at about 4:45 P.M., the employee was abruptly notified that he was suspended without pay, and ordered to get out and stay out. After he had fretted for some days or weeks, charges would be delivered. After more weeks and months, with the employee's savings melting away, the case would grind to a conclusion. We have graphic descriptions of the effect of this treatment on the employee's morale, in cases that contained not a suggestion of imminent risk. The whole business was so unnecessarily callous that I suspect it must have been intended, in some agencies, to force the employee to resign.[19]

It should be added that the frequency with which the government was forced to pay back salary when investigation was completed tends to confirm the inefficiency of the program and the hair-trigger reaction of administrators to the first word of rumor against a once-trusted employee.[20] But this type of atonement fails to account for the number of employees who were discharged, or who otherwise retired, because of the hypersuspicion which saturated the program in some agencies. And an award of back salary does not dissolve the distress of those who were subject to the program. Knowing his own innocence, as the Navy also should have known it, Abraham Chasanow has stated:

Insofar as the effect of such experience is concerned, I'm afraid I cannot adequately portray what being suspended or fired as a security risk does to a person and his family. My description of the experience as a nightmare is an understatement. My wife and I each lost almost 10 pounds the first few days after I was suspended. I don't know how much more weight we lost after I was

[19] Ralph S. Brown, *Loyalty and Security*, 300. Quoted by courtesy of the Yale University Press.

[20] *Report* of the Johnston Committee, 167; *Hearings* before the Johnston Committee, 967–968.

fired. We didn't have a single good night's sleep in the 13 months between my suspension and reinstatement. I am sure 13 months in prison, or in solitary confinement, would not have been as difficult to live through. I was afraid it would ruin our children's lives and futures. I was afraid to associate with others, for fear they would in turn be branded as security risks through their association with me. I knew that the public considered the term "security risk" synonymous with "traitor." I also knew that I had never done anything which could remotely justify the charge that I was a "security risk," even in its narrowest sense. When I decided to fight for reinstatement, even if it took the rest of my life, I was not particularly concerned about getting my job back. I was fighting for my honor and that of my family. I was fighting to regain the good reputation we were fortunate enough to have had. I was fighting to prove how terribly wrong it was to call me a security risk. I do not think anyone who has not been branded a security risk can fully appreciate the emotional strain we endured for 13 months. I think we ran the entire gamut of emotions. It was only our confidence in ultimate justice, and the encouragement of our friends and neighbors, and the support of the press which enabled us to endure it.[21]

Chasanow was suspended without notice on unsupported charges after twenty-two years in the Navy Hydrographic Office; the Navy required a leisurely thirteen months to discover the error of mind which wove fact and fancy into the characteristic robe of conspiracy.

This combination of urgency and delay is typical of many government security operations. The middle ground, until recent reforms were made in some agencies, was seldom explored.[22] The Passport Office of the Department of State

[21] *Hearings* before the Johnston Committee, 626–627.

[22] See, for example, the Navy's admission of error and changes in their security program after the Chasanow debacle, *ibid.*, 616–621.

was justly charged by the Wright Commission with "delays ranging from several months to more than a year," and these were "the rule rather than the exception." [23] Administrative inefficiency was not always the cause of unreasonable delay. There is some evidence that delay was used in the issuance of passports to wear down the applicant or with the hope that the troublesome problem might dissolve spontaneously. The behavior of the Department of State in the Kamen, Nathan, and Pauling cases suggests this, and William Worthy, the newsman who dared to enter Communist China without the approval of the Department of State, contends that his requests for a new passport met with the tactic of "under advisement," [24] a well-known bureaucratic euphemism for conscious procrastination. Urgency, on the other hand, when called for, quickly displaced delay. The suspensions under the loyalty and security programs were effected with headlong dispatch, and the Immigration and Naturalization Service frequently rushed the departure of unwanted visitors or denaturalized citizens. The quick trip of William Heikkila to Finland was sponsored by the Immigration and Naturalization authorities. He was deported without adequate funds, baggage, or notice to his wife or lawyer.[25] These instances are not isolated examples of the

[23] *Report of the Commission on Government Security* (1957), 493.

[24] *Hearings before the Subcommittee on Constitutional Rights of the (Senate) Committee on the Judiciary*, 85th Cong., 1st Sess., "The Right to Travel" (1958), pt. 1, p. 27. For other passport cases see the same Committee, *Hearings*, 84th Cong., 2d Sess., "Security and Constitutional Rights," *passim*, and *Freedom to Travel: Report of the Special Committee to Study Passport Procedures of the Association of the Bar of the City of New York* (New York, 1958).

[25] *New York Times*, April 22, 23, 24, 25, 1958; Jack Wasserman, "Some Defects in the Administration of Our Immigration Laws," *Law and Contemporary Problems*, 21: 376–381 (Spring, 1956). For evi-

conflict between administrative eagerness and constitutional sensibility.

The withering of decency and common sense is often found embedded in excessive legalism. The current reliance on legalism fails to distinguish between what is legal and what is wise; while, perhaps paradoxically, legalism has led to the denial of due process of law in executive operations. Administrative convenience has dictated a reliance on "legality" of restrictive measures and decisions and on the "legality" of administering security programs without due process of law.

The Department of Defense, for example, has the legal right to withhold mountains of information; no government employee has the right to continued employment if he is a security risk; and there is, at present, no doubt as to the legal right of the government to deport an alien to Communist China. On the other hand, the wisdom of withholding information which will aid science, the wisdom of discharging a loyal employee with distant relatives behind the Iron Curtain (a security risk), or the wisdom of deporting to Communist China an alien who might be subject to persecution is, to say the least, doubtful. As Justice Douglas remarked in dissenting against such a deportation:

---

dence that an excess of tears was shed in the press over Mr. Heikkila see the *Hearings before a Subcommittee of the (House) Committee on the Judiciary,* 85th Cong., 2d Sess., "Judicial Review of Deportation and Exclusion Orders" (1958), pp. 23–31; *Annual Report of the Immigration and Naturalization Service,* 1957, pp. 13–14. The fact remains that until the law is changed a constitutional system permits an individual to exhaust all legal remedies; and in other cases, if not this one, the Service has failed frequently to meet its own admirable test of administering the law "with common sense and compassion" (*New York Times,* April 25, 1958).

I would not read the law narrowly to make it the duty of our officials to send this alien and the others in the companion case to what may be persecution or death. Technicalities need not enmesh us. The spirit of the law provides the true guide.[26]

As for due process of law, security proceedings for government employment may not require the right of the suspect to confront witnesses against him or access to a system of appeals, but wisdom and decency require the elements of a fair hearing.[27]

In a word, the executive branch, with the comfort of the legalist's self-deception, has confused the substance of justice

[26] Dissenting opinion in *Leng May Ma v. Barber,* 357 U.S. 185, 192 (1958).

[27] An interesting example of legalism in action, albeit with a happy ending, is the Mezei case. An alien who had lived in the United States for twenty-five years, Mezei visited Romania to see his dying mother. He was refused the right to re-enter the United States and was held on Ellis Island for two years while the Department of Justice (and the Supreme Court, 345 U.S. 216) determined that he was not entitled to due process. After the Department had won its case, the victory or a pang of conscience led to the appointment of an *ad hoc* committee which permitted Mezei to hear the evidence against him. It was found that he had been a member of the Communist party, but a favorable committee recommendation was accepted and Mezei returned to his home in Buffalo (Kenneth Culp Davis, "The Requirement of a Trial-Type Hearing," *Harvard Law Review,* 70: 251 [1956]). In the important case, *Greene v. McElroy,* 360 U.S. 474 (1959), the Court seemed to limit its holding to the deficiency in procedures (withdrawing security clearance from an employee of a business holding a government contract) because there was an absence of *explicit* authorization by Congress or the Executive to permit the Department of Defense to do so without the safeguards of confrontation or cross-examination; the Chief Justice, with characteristic expansiveness, seemed to condemn the validity of the procedures under any conditions, even if explicitly authorized. For the program subsequently proposed by the Eisenhower administration and permitting limited confrontation see the *New York Times,* Feb. 21, 1960.

and fair procedure with its legal right to deny both. The administrator may, thereby, protect himself from the courts —although even here the judiciary is increasingly severe —but not against the charge of contributing to the decay of constitutionalism.

The record, of course, is not one of unalleviated dreariness. The advances in the field of minority rights by means of the affirmative hand of administrative power will become evident in the pages that follow. As for the Bill of Rights, both President Truman and President Eisenhower have indicated dissatisfaction, and in some instances anger, about excesses within their own administration and political party. President Truman, after an evening conference at Blair House with individuals outside the government who were concerned about the excesses of the loyalty program, requested that his staff look further into the matter. The President remarked, "I have been very much disturbed with the action of some of these [loyalty] Boards and I want to find some way to put a stop to their un-American activities." Both Cold War Presidents and officials in the White House office moved, however sporadically, to modify some of the harmful acts of their subordinates; and although it is impossible to find a sustained pattern of self-generated reform within the executive branch, efforts were made to take account of past error in formulating new programs.[28] President Truman's distaste for the loyalty-security program

[28] President Truman to Charles S. Murphy, June 24, 1951, Harry S. Truman Papers, Truman Library, Independence, Mo. See the *Report* of the Johnston Committee, pt. 10; *Twenty-seventh Report by the (House) Committee on Government Operations*, 85th Cong., 2d Sess., "Availability of Information from Federal Departments and Agencies" (1958), pt. 4; *New York Times*, Feb. 21, 1960.

and President Eisenhower's warning that his security program must not be abused may seem in retrospect largely ineffectual, but it is necessary to speculate about the degree of excess had they not spoken or had they emphasized the security aspects alone.

In the same way an underlying loyalty to individual rights broke through the administrative pattern when in the so-called "guilt by relationship" cases (as in the Chasanow case) service Secretaries in the Department of Defense stepped forward to counteract the senseless zeal of their security officers.[29] The admission by the Department of Justice in argument before the Supreme Court that there was a "right to travel" may have been dictated by anticipation of the Court's sentiments, but it was, nonetheless, a significant official assertion of an important aspect of liberty. The self-denial of the FBI at important points in recent history,[30] Harold Stassen's common-sense solution of the Ladejinsky problem by hiring the "security risk" out from under the Department of Agriculture, and the well-constructed security program of the Atomic Energy Commission combine with certain decisions of the Immigration and Naturalization Service and the declassification of documents by the Department of Defense to confirm the existence of a stubborn, if somewhat muted, loyalty to individual liberties even in the worst years.

The predominant pattern, nevertheless, embodies the administrative attitudes mentioned above. All, from the presumption of validity for "security" measures to excessive

[29] Especially Secretaries Finletter, Talbott, and Thomas. See Brown, *Loyalty and Security,* 272.

[30] Don Whitehead, *The FBI Story* (New York, 1956), 203–204.

95

legalism, developed into a system of preventive law which is deeply embedded in institutional practices and thereby constitutes a primary obstacle to reform.[31] Punishment before the commission of an unlawful act, or before clear evidence of a conspiracy exists, is implicit, for example, in the personnel security program, many passport denials, and some operations of the Post Office Department. It is reinforced by the administrative acceptance of the virtue of its own efforts. However necessary preventive law may be in some cases, it produces built-in resistance to change. The presumption of validity, once established, is difficult to overtake with a presumption of invalidity for governmental restraints. When decency withers, and indecency is profitable, it is hard to impose another pattern. Excessive legalism and 100 per cent security are safe in their own logic, and broad and irresponsible use of discretion, gaining over the years institutionalized trappings, has an imperial life all its own.

The courts may continue to attack the procedural shortcomings and Congress may become aroused periodically, but it will require the sustained use of the instruments of the presidency to change the pattern of excessive dependence on preventive law.

The Appointing Power

The administrative instruments which enable the President to promote and protect individual liberties need not

[31] See John Lord O'Brian, *National Security and Individual Freedom* (Cambridge, 1955), 22–25, and the excellent discussion of preventive law by Cornelius P. Cotter and J. Malcolm Smith, "Freedom and Authority in the Amphibial State," *Midwest Journal of Political Science,* 1: 40–59 (May, 1957). See also Benjamin Ginsburg, *Rededication to Freedom* (New York, 1959).

be invented. The last decade provides both instructive proof that they exist and a fund of experience with their use and misuse. The point which needs emphatic acceptance is that direction, oversight, and the activation of these instruments must come from the highest levels of the executive departments and of the White House itself. Power, of course, must be delegated, although final supervision should never be. To pretend otherwise is to deny not only presidential responsibility but any hope for change in present administrative patterns. Prestige, power, and the weapons of persuasion, hampered as they may be by the obstacles spelled out above, reside with sufficient force only at the highest levels of the executive branch and, more often than not, in the hands of the President himself.

As chief administrator, the President possesses the power of appointment and removal and the opportunity to see that administrative discretion is used creatively rather than destructively. He can issue executive orders and statements of presidential purpose, and he can demand, if not always receive, obedience and information from within his own household. Charged by the Constitution with the duty to see to the faithful execution of the laws, the President can do much to assure that procedures and intent of executive action favor and extend individual liberties, not diminish them.

Whether acting in his executive capacity or as commander in chief or as ceremonial head of the nation, the President's temperament and the atmosphere in the White House will help to shape the attitudes in the Federal administrative structure. The willingness of the President to accept a degree of risk in the interests of due process of law and free speech, while demanding a pattern of positive action to protect minority rights, will influence, if never completely dominate, the decisions of his subordinates. By statement and example he can assure his own administrators that courage and imagination will be rewarded and that each will be defended by the President himself against congressional or public criticism.

Today, in sum, if individual liberties are to thrive, the President cannot escape the obligation to sustain and support, if not frequently initiate, constructive proposals and courageous administrative action. Without his interest, administrators will have little incentive to break with some of the more damaging aspects of preventive law.

Clearly, the President's span of attention and control is limited in this field as it is in others. For this reason alone it is essential that primary attention be given to the quality of governmental personnel. With this the nation's chief investigative officer agrees. J. Edgar Hoover has remarked:

We can have the Constitution, the best laws in the land, and the most honest reviews by the courts—but unless the law enforcement profession is steeped in the democratic tradition, maintains the highest ethics, and makes its work a career of honor, civil liberties will continually—and without end—be violated.[32]

With regard to investigative personnel, Hoover speaks from experience dating back to World War I when the FBI had the standards of a low-grade private detective agency. A low point in government personnel policy was reached with the founding of the American Protective League during the Red Scare of World War I. Governmentally sponsored,

[32] J. Edgar Hoover, "Civil Liberties and Law Enforcement: "The Role of the FBI," *Iowa Law Review,* 37: 179 (Winter, 1952).

the League was an association of private citizens who wore an official badge styling them Auxiliaries of the Department of Justice, thus giving official sanction to their efforts to ferret out a wide range of "anti-Americans."

The effect of this kind of amateurism in investigative work is reflected in the more recent crash program of hiring to meet the demands of loyalty-security programs after 1948. Too frequently second-rate collection agents and private detectives or discards from other agencies were given the responsibility to determine the security standing of their fellow employees. In contrast—and contrary to the liberal myth—it is significant that the FBI has an impressively clean record in such activity. It is particularly impressive when one considers the explosive material with which the FBI must deal. Professionalism, then, in a "career with honor" should be the first insistence of the chief executive in investigative appointments. Well trained, restrained by the limits of their own professional competence, and controlled by superiors who use the investigative report with knowledge of its limitations, the professional will do less damage to liberty than the energetic amateur. Technical competence, while restricted in vision and dangerous if counterweights are not applied, is a minor threat when compared to the expansive and politically conditioned zeal of the nonprofessional.

When one advances to the level of evaluation and policy formulation, technical competence is not enough to satisfy the demands of liberty. For there the administrative personality comes in contact with the uncertainties inherent in any attempt to find the proper mixture of liberty and restraint. How decide whether nudist magazines should be

banned from the mails or the unexpurgated *Lady Chatterley's Lover* from entry through the customs; how decide
whether past association with an organization on the Attorney General's list is current evidence of future disloyalty;
or, in another case, how decide the government's policy
concerning segregation in the armed forces or in Federal
installations in the South? These are or have been subtle
questions of judgment,[33] and the "science" of public administration provides no universal guideline. It is in this
sphere of decision making that the temperament of the
administrator may become a crucial factor in molding the
governmental response.

Unfortunately, it is impossible to delineate with any accuracy the temperament which is most sympathetic to individual liberties. It may be found in the administrator
who is inclined to come to the defense of the one against
the many and of the person against the impersonality of
modern bureaucracy. It is, perhaps, part of the individual's
sense of injustice which is at least "the capacity to recognize
oppression of another as a species of attack upon himself"; [34] or it may be an elemental restlessness which is cre-

[33] Huntington Cairns recalls that after his appointment as an adviser
to the Treasury on Customs Bureau exclusion of material from abroad
he spoke with a customs inspector to determine the standards which
had been followed in excluding books. The inspector used *Ulysses* as
an example, saying that he came upon it because it was heavy and had
paper covers. Upon opening the volume, ordered by an actress, he saw
some "very dirty words" and refused delivery. The inspector's sub-
jective standard of judgment became evident when the actress requested to examine the volume. He asked if she were married, and
when she replied that she was not, he remarked, "Lady, I ain't even
going to let you look at it" (Huntington Cairns to the author, July 16,
1959).

[34] Edmond N. Cahn, *The Sense of Injustice* (New York, 1949), 25.

ated (even in the face of apparent self-interest and convenience) when liberty is threatened, when government policy undercuts rights which were thought to be an unassailable part of every man's freedom. It may appear when, beyond political advantage, the enthusiasm of moral purpose attaches to the activities of the Federal executive in combating discrimination—but in defense of the individual, not an abstract racial group. And it is immanent in the prudence with which all power should be exercised.

Indeed, these elusive administrative qualities exist only in a statement of the ideal. But for those key appointments where decisions can have a vital effect on individual liberties it will pay the appointing authority to search for them and to see that these men attempt to spread their standards to the least administrator in the agency. It is helpful if the person carries with him, particularly at the higher levels, prestige and a sense of independence which may enable him to deny immediate ambitions while he withstands the pressure of an unpopular decision. At all levels, the administrator who is free of the stultifying ideologies of the right or the left may avoid smothering the interest of the individual in doctrine. Education rather than mere training is a prerequisite. We know little of the security officers under the Eisenhower and Truman administrations; the scattered evidence emerging from their proceedings suggests, however, that in the early stages, at least, they had a working knowledge of popular un-Americanism but understood little of Marxism, of left-wing movements in this country, and of history.[35] The list of volumes proscribed by the Post Office Department continues to reflect a limited understanding of literary values, and the restrictions on scientific informa-

[35] Brown, *Loyalty and Security*, 27–28.

tion upheld by the executive branch exalt secrecy rather than the free flow of ideas.

Education, or a sense of perspective in constitutional values and history, tends to carry with it an openness of mind and a willingness to be inconsistent; it may inculcate caution and skepticism about government restrictions and encourage the constitutionalist's conviction that "claims in the name of security [and political advantage] are not to be automatically honored." [36] The ideal appointee would be, for want of a better word, tough, not with the toughness associated with the stereotype of the security officer or the "practical" administrator but with the intellectual toughness needed when the certainties of the automatic decision for security are exchanged for the uncertainties of a finding in the direction of individual liberty. Those dealing with minority rights, in turn, although knowing the technical aspects of their role, are most valuable when accepting the efficacy and necessity of positive government action against discrimination. It should not be necessary to add that in all cases energy and purposiveness will enliven administrative thinking about these goals.

These intangible qualities lie behind the general descriptive phrases heard so often when the government's handling of individual liberties is discussed. It may be a call for "common-sense judgment," "judicial attitudes," or "administration with a heart." President Eisenhower called it "fair play."

I was raised in a little town of which most of you have never heard. But in the West it is a famous place. It is called Abilene. Kansas. We had as our Marshal for a long time a man named

[36] *Ibid.*, 478.

Wild Bill Hickok. If you don't know anything about him, read your Westerns more. Now that town had a code, and I was raised as a boy to prize that code. It was: meet anyone face to face with whom you disagree. You could not sneak up on him from behind, or do any damage to him, without suffering the penalty of an outraged citizenry. If you met him face to face and took the same risks he did, you could get away with almost anything, as long as the bullet was in the front.[37]

Maxwell Rabb, who, as one of President Eisenhower's major advisers on civil rights, knew much of individual liberty matters from the perspective of the White House, describes the temperament of those sensitive to invasions of the rights of others as the possession of "decent men," dedicated to security but "upset by injustice and open to argument." [38]

Needless to say, short of the introduction of a system of Platonic guardians, it will never be possible to saturate an administration with men holding such attitudes. Individuals embracing them in proper measure are rare, the existence and constancy of the temperament is difficult to predict, and other administrative qualities, such as *expertise* in the job at hand, will take precedence. There are, nevertheless, certain measures which can be taken. First among them is the aura of expectations which surrounds the White House. Administrators will tend to respond in tune with the White House and, knowing that violations of the substance of the Bill of Rights or discrimination will be frowned upon, will inhibit those administrators who would damage individual rights and encourage those who wish to move in a liberal

[37] Address to B'nai B'rith, Washington, D.C., Nov. 23, 1953, cited by Justice Frankfurter in *Jay* v. *Boyd*, 351 U.S. 372 (1956).
[38] Interview with Maxwell M. Rabb, April 8, 1958.

direction. Second, training *and* education in the necessities of constitutionalism as well as security will have its effect.[39] And, finally, although it is impossible to make the appointee's constitutional sense a factor in each case, it is possible to establish centers of conscience at the higher administrative level. Today, the positions which affect individual liberties most directly are those of the Secretaries and Undersecretaries in the Departments of State, Defense, and Justice and those in such specific agencies as the Civil Service Commission, the Passport Office of the Department of State, the Bureau of Immigration and Naturalization, and the FBI, not to mention the White House staff itself. It goes without saying that Federal judges and district attorneys share a crucial role. Men with proper attitudes in these key positions, once given the backing of the President, can do much to instruct and restrain their subordinates. A creed which is easily adapted to all of these positions was voiced by Francis Biddle soon after his appointment as Attorney General:

[39] As the Johnston Committee reported (p. 165): "The personnel security officer should be a most carefully selected and trained person. Not only because of the tremendous power he wields over the lives and careers, both present and future, of individuals, but also because of the vague, general, and indeterminate elements of the Executive Order No. 10450, especially the security risk criteria. Therefore, in reaching a fair determination it is necessary for those engaged in the security program to be persons professionally trained and competent in several fields. This should include a thorough knowledge of the current national security problem; he should also be versed in law, political science, psychology, philosophy, history, and a general knowledge of subversive organizations and their methods of operation. . . . The personnel security officer holds an unenviable position, not only because of his task, but very often he is looked upon by other employees as somewhat less than competent."

As chief legal officer of the Government, I realize fully the immense task which rests on me, a duty which must be accepted without faltering and daily exercised—the obligation of affording leadership by speech, by example, and above all by consistent action in the field of law enforcement and protection of our rights, of the great group of civil rights, built up so laboriously over the centuries.[40]

Biddle's appointment and subsequent record, aided by Roosevelt's determination to avoid a recurrence in World War II of the illiberal experiences of World War I, proved the value of presidential foresight. Then, as now, it would be unrealistic to expect an appointment, made in a time of competing urgencies, to be on this basis alone. Nevertheless, it is within the power, and it is part of the administrative obligation, of the chief executive and of those who appoint in his name to insist that concern for constitutional rights be a significant qualification for holding some offices. It is especially in those agencies where such rights are most directly affected. Above all, the point of view should be represented in the White House. The President's appointing power may be used to place at least one man near the President who will keep the President informed about his own administration's shortcomings and the nation's state of mind about constitutional rights. In the Roosevelt, Truman, and Eisenhower administrations individuals were specifically appointed to handle minority problems, and others were self-appointed guardians of First Amendment freedoms and due process of law. In the Roosevelt administration, Mrs.

[40] Speech to the Brooklyn Bar Association, Feb. 5, 1942, in Department of Justice Files.

Roosevelt, James Rowe, and David Niles (and Harold Ickes and Francis Biddle in the Cabinet) were in a position to alert the President to a variety of threats to constitutional rights; in the Truman administration, David Niles, and later Philleo Nash, among several others, made an aware President even more aware of the requirements of the Bill of Rights; in the Eisenhower administration the responsibility fell to Maxwell Rabb.

Many others played the same role, depending upon the issue or the personal inclination of the President, but these names stand out.[41] Either because of personal conscience or by reason of political service to the President, each attempted to post watch over constitutional rights in the President's name. All did so with varying degrees of success and each in a slightly different manner. Mrs. Roosevelt, for example, eased the way for Negro leaders who wished to see the President and alerted the President to the unhappy situation of the Japanese-American evacuees in World War II; Philleo Nash dealt generally with minority problems

[41] That the "institutionalization" of this function is not as important as the constitutional sensibility of the individual coming in contact with the President is illustrated by one account of an Army proposal immediately before World War II for blanket military censorship in the event of war. Lowell Mellett, then director of Government Reports, was called to the White House by President Roosevelt and handed an Army document outlining the plan. The President asked what he was to do with it. "You can't possibly approve of it," Mellett replied. "First of all, you don't believe in it. But more important, if press censorship occurs, we'd never get out from under it." The President agreed but said that he had to answer it. Again he asked what he could do. "Lose it," Mellett replied. The President called in his press secretary directing him to do just that. Nothing further was heard of the proposal. The facts are a recollection of Thomas G. Corcoran. See the *Washington Post and Times Herald,* April 11, 1960.

and was apparently largely responsible for gathering the administrative and political force which resulted in President Truman's Committee on Civil Rights; others reminded the President of the dangers to the Bill of Rights implicit in the loyalty-security program and the flood of internal security proposals in the early 1950's; and, if any one person can be given credit, Maxwell Rabb used the prestige of the White House to bring an end to blatant and officially sanctioned segregation in the District of Columbia and in Federal military facilities in the South.

One function of any White House assistant is to protect the President from what he does not want to do or cannot do. But those who are appointed as advisers on minority affairs or who, in the course of their work on any policy matter, find that presidential action or inaction may affect constitutional rights may serve also to inform the President as to what he can or should do. It is essentially a triple responsibility shared by all men, public or private, who are close to the President, and it was fulfilled to a lesser or greater degree by men like Nash and Rabb during their time in the White House. First, these men may act as points of contact between the White House and individuals inside and outside the government who may wish to communicate with the President on matters involving constitutional rights; second, driven by their own sense of constitutional duty or the political implications of the question, they may see that the information, or information gathered by them independently, gets to the President or that the matter is dealt with effectively otherwise; third, supported by the President's interest and backing, they may work with government agencies and representatives of extragovernmental groups to bring about a favorable change in public policy. What "the White House wants" and what "the President wishes me to say" are powerful weapons against the excesses of the police mentality or violations of Negro rights. By making information available to the President and the President available to interested persons, by initiating studies within the White House, or by conferences and phone calls trying to break down the particularism or lethargy of government agencies, these appointees can do much to make constitutional rights a persistent policy factor in the busy world of a presidential day. To those interested groups outside the government, such a person may be known as "a friend" in the White House; to agency heads, an opponent of their administrative convenience; and to the President or the other members of the White House staff an individual who predictably raises the issue of individual liberty when policy matters are under consideration. If the President is to fulfill his responsibility to constitutional rights, the encouragement of this function and the appointment of such men cannot be overlooked.

Finally, the appointing power, together with the removal power, can carry considerable symbolic force. The appointment of Scott McLeod as security officer in the Department of State, given his reputed attachment to McCarthyism, became a symbol of the Eisenhower administration's rigorous attitude toward "security." His transfer to the post of ambassador to Ireland was similarly interpreted as a symbolic withdrawal from the attitudes which McLeod had come to represent for the administration. The appointment in 1934 of Huntington Cairns as a special legal adviser to the Treasury department not only affected the substance of

Customs Bureau decisions on what constitutes art but has exemplified the Bureau's concern for art's legitimate claims,[42] and the appointment of Negroes to important posts signifies executive attention to minority rights. J. Ernest Wilkins was appointed Assistant Secretary of Labor and later to the Commission on Civil Rights by President Eisenhower; a Negro held the ambassadorship to Rumania in 1958; and within the post-World War II period Ralph Bunche's distinguished career in foreign affairs, the appointment of the first Negro to a Court of Appeals judgeship, and the appointment of a Negro to the White House staff marked the entry of the Negro minority into responsible governmental positions.[43] Today, according to a government survey,[44] one out of four positions in the Federal government in Washington is held by a Negro, although most of these are custodial for other minor positions. In the South, however (the claims of some sanguine administrators to the contrary), discrimination in employment within the Federal establishment is still the common pattern.[45]

The removal power (or it may take the form of denial of a promotion) is a weapon now being used with greater frequency where violations of minority rights are concerned. In

[42] For the Cairns appointment and his influence see Zechariah Chafee, *Government and Mass Communications* (Chicago, 1947), 254–275.

[43] "The People Take the Lead," *Report of the American Jewish Committee,* 1958, p. 12; C. Vann Woodward, *The Strange Career of Jim Crow* (New York, 1957), 122; *United States News and World Report,* Nov. 28, 1958.

[44] *Second Report of the President's Committee on Government Employment Policy* (1958), 9–10.

[45] For this discouraging side of the story see William Peters, *The Southern Temper* (New York, 1959), ch. xv.

1948 the Secretary of the Treasury removed a collector of internal revenue in Alabama for his refusal to comply with a presidential order ending discrimination in government employment. In addition, the President's Committee on Government Employment Policy reports the following:

A defense establishment found that a supervisor in a field organization had practised racial discrimination in his promotional policy. The complainant was given the next available promotion, and the supervisor was transferred to a nonsupervisory position. A bureau of one of the major departments found that the superintendent of one of its training schools had disrupted the morale of his staff by discriminatory remarks and actions. The superintendent was dismissed from his job.[46]

Where there have been violations of due process of law or the spirit of the First Amendment by administrators, on the contrary, 100 per cent pursuit of the strictest canons of "security-mindedness" usually has been equated with 100 per cent job security. It is interesting to speculate on the manifold improvement if the threat of removal or denial of promotion were used against those who overclassify documents or who ignorantly and arbitrarily deny the privilege of the mails to nonpornographic material. As one witness before a Senate committee investigating the personnel security program remarked:

The fact that a security officer can point to so many undeniable security risks as having been detected does not prove that he has executed his job as he should have. If he cannot also show that

[46] *Second Report of the President's Committee,* 18; "The People Take the Lead," 7.

he has also protected the innocent, then he must be replaced and someone found who can perform both functions.[47]

Doubtless such a refreshing change will not come quickly; but although the power has rarely been used for this purpose, it should be emphasized that it is still a part of the President's arsenal.

Executive Directives

Once given personnel in key positions who have both the time and the inclination to react constructively to individual liberties problems as they arise, and once given presidential willingness to lead and participate in establishing the proper climate of opinion, there are several other instruments of persuasion and direction available. Whatever the specific means—whether by executive order, by directives from the White House or department heads, or by means of the oversight and persuasion of presidential committees—the process is essentially the same: the introduction of a higher standard of performance by means of official command or authoritative suggestion.

As recent experience proves, this type of executive weapon can be used to extinguish rather than sustain constitutional rights. It is only necessary to reflect on the destructive application of administrative directives. Presidential orders established the loyalty-security program, departmental orders amplified restrictions on passports, and executive pronouncements intensified the built-in secretiveness of Federal agencies. There are instances in the record, nevertheless, which

[47] *Hearings* before the Johnston Committee, 172. For an account of the demise of one security officer see the testimony of Louis J. Lyell, Clarence E. Clarke, and George V. McDavitt, in *ibid.*

point to the potential for constructive action by means of this type of administrative direction. To cite only a few examples: Harry Truman's attempt to establish the Nimitz Commission on Internal Security and Individual Rights to study the loyalty-security program failed because of congressional opposition; but he countered by utilizing the National Security Council's Interdepartmental Committee on Government Security. In the same way, President Eisenhower attempted to remove some of the worst blemishes from his security program when, after the embarrassment of the Ladejinsky case, the Personnel Advisory Committee was established in the White House under the chairmanship of Thomas J. Donegan. Studies have been initiated in other agencies by presidential or departmental direction to change past practices infringing on individual liberty, including violations of due process of law. In some cases (for example, establishment of the Board of Passport Appeals and the diminished use of secret evidence by the Immigration and Naturalization Service) remedies followed pressure from the Federal courts, but the essential point, nonetheless, is that even here moves were made by unilateral executive action.[48]

Administrative directives or specific expressions of sentiment by the White House can be used to relax excessive suspiciousness and to prevent the improper use of administrative discretion. Such action may, in some instances, amount to direct presidential intervention. The White House may not succeed in turning back a headlong administrative or

[48] Harry S. Truman, *Memoirs: Years of Trial and Hope* (New York, 1956), 288–289; *Hearings* before the Johnston Committee, testimony of Thomas J. Donegan, 872–887; remarks of Congressman John V. Lindsay, *Congressional Record* (daily ed.), April 27, 1959, App. 3485.

national trend, but the possibility of failure should not vitiate the attempt. An illustration of direct presidential involvement is mentioned by Harry Truman in his *Memoirs*. Although the unimpressive record of most of the Truman Attorneys General in regard to positive protection of individual liberties would suggest that the quality of the appointee rather than general statements of presidential intent is the critical factor, the following account is illustrative of one President's sensitivity to individual liberties:

When I conferred with Clark regarding his appointment, I expressed to him my ideas of how I wanted him to run the Department of Justice. I emphasized to him the need to be vigilant to maintain the rights of individuals under the provisions of the Bill of Rights. I asked him to call a meeting of the district attorneys of the United States. *I told them, when we met,* that while they were enforcement officers of the government it was their duty to see also that rights of the citizens were protected. I pointed out the danger of prosecuting officers becoming persecuting officers. They are there not only for the purpose of enforcing the law in the interest of the government of the United States, but also to be sure that the rights of individuals under the Constitution are fully protected. I emphasized this so much that Tom Clark thought I was "hipped" on the subject—and I was.[49]

Although administrative directives of the Truman type seemed to have had only a limited effect on the massive apathy toward due process of law and First Amendment freedoms in the depths of the 1950's, administrative orders and presidential direction, in contrast, produced a series of modest revolutions in the government's attitude toward dis-

[49] Harry S. Truman, *Memoirs: Year of Decisions* (New York, 1955), 325–326. Copyright 1955, Time Inc. Emphasis supplied.

crimination. The experience in recent years with the systematic use of administrative orders and persuasion to encourage social change provides dramatic evidence of the significance of this executive instrument. This generation is witnessing the overthrow of a tradition of official acceptance of discrimination and segregation and the emergence of its opposite: the acceptance of official responsibility for the reduction of violations of minority rights by means of sustained application of the executive power. The consequences of vigorous presidential action were felt in the continuing campaign against racial discrimination in Federal employment and in Federal facilities throughout the country. Within the last generation administrative power, free of the encumbrances of congressional involvement, brought about the desegregation of the armed forces, while an increasingly vigorous attack was made on discrimination by firms enjoying contracts with the Federal government. These developments are due almost entirely to the determination of three Presidents—Roosevelt, Truman, and Eisenhower.

A major phase in this administrative revolution was completed when the Department of Defense announced in June, 1955, that segregation in the armed forces was at an end, an event which one military historian describes as "probably the one most influential single step toward the increasing recognition of the Negro citizen's right to full status as a human being." [50] There is no need to retrace here the long and tortuous path of this advance for the Negro.[51] What is of signifi-

[50] Walter Millis, *Individual Freedom and the Common Defense* (New York, 1957), 18.

[51] Lee Nichols, *Breakthrough on the Color Front* (New York, 1954), *passim*. See also Peters, *The Southern Temper*, 139–145, for a summary of the "secret" report, "Project Clear."

cance for present purposes is the effect of presidential attitudes and those of the service Secretaries. The formal steps
toward desegregation are found in a bundle of executive
orders, an investigation by a presidential Committee on
Equality of Treatment in the Armed Forces (1948–1950),
and numerous studies by other groups within the Department of Defense. Behind the formalities lie the interplay of
prejudice and service tradition, the fear of congressional reprisal, and the power of the Negro vote.[52]

President Roosevelt engineered the first experimental
moves in desegregation. Always cautious about such matters,
he was limited, too, by his own fear of disrupting morale during wartime and the unimaginative opposition of Secretaries
Knox and Stimson. The President spoke out against discrimination in the treatment of Negro troops. He attacked the
traditional policy of assigning Negroes to menial tasks and
encouraged the training of Negro units in the specialities of
war. And although he did little more, his political responsive-
ness and sense of decency on such matters contributed to the
first fissures in an established American tradition.[53]

The shattering of the tradition awaited the appearance of
the period of postwar sensitivity to civil rights, more enlightened attitudes in the Department of Defense, and—of
crucial importance—emphatic presidential support. Both

[52] See A Report by the President's Committee on Equality of Treatment in the Armed Services, "Freedom to Serve" (Washington, 1950).
For the political implications of desegregation see Nichols, Breakthrough on the Color Front, 84–88.

[53] Nichols, Breakthrough on the Color Front, chs. i–viii; Henry L.
Stimson and McGeorge Bundy, On Active Service in Peace and War
(New York, 1947), 461–464; the President's press conference, Feb. 5,
1944, Franklin D. Roosevelt Papers, Roosevelt Library, Hyde Park,
N.Y.

President Truman and President Eisenhower gave full backing and no little direction to their service Secretaries. Secretary Stuart Symington utilized presidential support in his successful program of desegregation for the Air Force. As he told his subordinates, "We're going to end segregation. Those are my orders from the Commander-in-Chief. You've got to stop the double talk and act." [54] The determination of men such as Symington, James Forrestal, and Robert B. Anderson, assisted by the directives of the commander in chief, led to desegregation of personnel in the Air Force and the Navy. The same determination, coupled with the pressure of manpower needs in combat, produced desegregation in Korea and by 1955 in the entire Army. The need for efficiency in the armed forces, a military desideratum which segregation threatened, took precedence over any abstract moral argument and helped to discourage outright congressional opposition. But for each step forward success hinged on the insistence of the commander in chief.

Closely tied to desegregation in the armed forces was the companion policy to end segregation in schools on military posts and in Federal facilities generally. The Truman administration, although somewhat laggard in terminating segregation in Federal facilities in the South (particularly those of the Navy), did end segregation in schools under the control of the Department of Defense. President Eisenhower, after announcing that there would be no segregation where Federal defense funds were involved, brought about an end to official acceptance of segregation among civilian employees in the sixty Navy installations in the South, including the Charleston and Norfolk navy yards. The Navy, having once

[54] Nichols, *Breakthrough on the Color Front,* 79.

116

defended its inaction with the argument that it should not be called upon to solve problems which it did not create, shifted its position under White House direction.[55] This example of Federal leadership holds true for all the armed services, for such Federal agencies as the Veterans Administration, for licensing and concession agreements involving the use of land administered by some Federal departments, and for nonsegregated seating at service-academy athletic contests. The policy against segregation is established and represents a shift of some magnitude in officially supported values. Furthermore, this shift was accomplished solely by means of the President's constitutional powers as chief administrator and commander of the armed forces. The continuing problem is to guard against backsliding and to bolster halfhearted administration with presidential determination.

Unfinished Business

"In its many capacities," Richard M. Nixon once remarked, "[as] military commander, purchaser, employer, and lender of funds—the Government has found rich opportunities to effect far-reaching changes during the past ten years." [56] As military commander success is an accomplished fact; as lender of funds, purchaser, and employer considerable executive vigor and experimentation lie ahead.

The acceptance of the principle of no discrimination in Federal employment was a long time in coming and required the efforts of two Democratic Presidents and one Republican

[55] See the President's statement announcing the end of segregation, *New York Times,* Nov. 12, 1953. But see also Peters, *The Southern Temper,* ch. xv.
[56] "The People Take the Lead," 5.

to begin to overcome the discriminatory policies encouraged by Woodrow Wilson. President Roosevelt spoke against discrimination in the recovery programs, although there is little evidence that attention was given to his warning or that he followed through administratively. The principle, nonetheless, was expressed here and in the antidiscrimination policy of the wartime FEPC. In an informal talk to WPA administrators as early as 1935 Roosevelt remarked:

We cannot discriminate in any of the work we are conducting either because of race, or religion, or politics. If anybody asks you to discriminate, you can tell them that the President of the United States gave direct orders that there is not to be any such discrimination.[57]

By executive order in 1948 President Truman established the Federal Fair Employment Board in the Civil Service Commission in order to add some sanction to his predecessor's sentiments. The White House was active in jogging agencies which resisted the policy of nondiscrimination, and the President personally encouraged the Board.[58] The prestige and effectiveness of this administrative effort were

[57] "Franklin D. Roosevelt and Civil Rights," A Study Prepared by the Legislative Reference Service, *Congressional Record*, June 18, 1957, App. 4840–4841; Peters, *The Southern Temper*, 243.

[58] Memorandum of Donald S. Dawson to David Niles, Dec. 12, 1950; Harry S. Truman to Harry B. Mitchell, Dec. 23, 1950; Memorandum for the President from Donald S. Dawson, Oct. 5, 1951. When the Veterans Administration refused to follow the Fair Employment Board's recommendation that two Negro lawyers be promoted, Dawson informed the President, "With your approval, I will call in the Veterans Administrator and tell him it is your wish that he should comply with the recommendation of the Fair Employment Board" (all in the Truman Papers).

heightened by President Eisenhower's appointment of a President's Committee on Government Employment Policy in 1955. Under this program the head of each agency was responsible for fulfilling the President's policy against discrimination in Federal employment. In addition to dealing with specific complaints the Committee held conferences and utilized its authority to make recommendations to individual agencies. Most important, the Committee was authorized to report directly to the President.[59]

Although these fair employment programs have had the effect of reducing discrimination in government hiring, much remains to be done in the way of implementing a principle which is now accepted officially. Federal agencies in Washington are hiring more Negroes, and all hire at least a few, if only as token appointments. It is now possible for Negroes to be appointed to the ranks of middle management, although most Negro employees in the government hold custodial jobs. This pattern is partly the result of the relative limits on the number of qualified Negroes; it is also a result of the myth which pretends that there are very few qualified Negroes. The circular effect of past discrimination policies, furthermore, has reduced incentive among Negroes by restricting the number and types of jobs available. In addition, it is always difficult for the highly qualified Negro to advance at the same rate within the government service as his white counterpart, and discrimination in apprentice or other training programs intensifies the disadvantage imposed by color. Consequently, the problem in Washington is now largely

[59] See the *First Report* and *Second Report* of the President's Committee on Government Employment Policy.

119

one of changing token acceptance to real acceptance, removing discrimination in training programs, and assuring equality in promotion policy regardless of color.

The pattern of fair employment in Washington is a promising one, but the degree of positive acceptance varies from agency to agency, both in Washington and in field agencies. For example, such agencies as the Departments of Defense, of Health, Education, and Welfare, and of Labor and the Public Housing Administration have records somewhat superior to the NLRB, the Department of Agriculture, and the Department of State. In the South, not surprisingly, racial discrimination in hiring and promotion predominates, even where educated and well-trained Negroes are involved. For example, in Atlanta, where in one year 573 graduate and undergraduate degrees were earned by Negroes, of the more than thirty major Federal agencies "only five had permanent Negro employees above the level of janitorial and labor services." According to a survey of Negro employment by the Federal government in the South (in which the Post Office Department seems to be something of an exception) few Negroes are hired for other than menial jobs.[60] The cumbersome procedure of appeals to the Fair Employment Board as well as the "rule of three" (which permits an employer to choose one of the first three on the civil service list submitted to him) allows discrimination to exist frequently unknown and infrequently challenged. But most important has been the absence of any concerted drive from the White House against these practices in the South.

As for the government's role as purchaser and lender of funds, the executive has moved more cautiously here than

[60] Peters, *The Southern Temper*, 244–250.

in the attack on other aspects of discrimination. Where there is expenditure of Federal money, there is no constitutional limit on the power of the executive branch to demand that the money be untainted by discrimination. But there have been underlying doubts about the wisdom of mixing social control and economic policy. Any attempt to stop discrimination by denying loans or Federal contracts when racial discrimination exists, it is argued, moves the executive branch on an uncharted course into the sphere of state power and private decision making. Further, the possibility of congressional reprisal is raised, and (when the program entails an essential governmental activity, such as military procurement contracts) administrators may be reluctant to complicate the primary purpose by introducing the issue of nondiscrimination. Consequently, the denial of funds or contracts in order to compel obedience to a policy of nondiscrimination has been used with great caution. The executive has placed major emphasis on persuasion and education, although in the attempt to end discrimination where mortgage guarantees through the FHA are involved the government has introduced a modest element of compulsion when state law bans on discrimination exist.[61]

For many years the policy of the executive branch toward government guarantees of mortgages was guided by the discriminatory theories of the National Association of Real Estate Boards. Only recently the government removed from the FHA manual directions advising against loans in areas where there were "incompatible racial and social groups." After *Shelley* v. *Kraemer* (1948) President Truman issued an order

[61] For further discussion of this type of presidential persuasion see pp. 208–211.

prohibiting loan guarantees on restrictive covenant housing, but lukewarm recognition of the Truman principle coupled with an unwillingness to control the policies of private builders has placed severe limits on Federal intervention. Thus, as late as 1958, President Eisenhower's administrator of the Housing and Home Finance Agency stated that the government's policy was to conform with local law, whether or not it prohibits discrimination.[62]

The Eisenhower administration, however, did contribute new momentum to compliance with nondiscrimination clauses in government contracts, although here, too, the executive has held outright compulsion in check. As with the desegregation of the armed forces, the seed of present policy was planted by the Roosevelt administration. The President responded to pressure from Negro groups, including a threatened march on Washington, by issuing Executive Order 8802 in 1941. The order established the Committee on Fair Employment Practices and required that all Federal defense contracts contain a stipulation obligating the contractor "not to discriminate against any worker because of race, creed, color, or national origin." The Committee itself had little power and relied largely on publicity until 1943, when more funds and a field staff were provided to advise employers and trade unions. Some 5,000 cases out of 13,000

[62] Walter White, *How Far the Promised Land* (New York, 1956), 131; Charles Abrams, "Bias in the Use of Governmental Regulatory Powers," *University of Chicago Law Review*, 20: 414–425 (Spring, 1953), and "What the President Could Do about School Desegregation," *Reporter*, Oct. 18, 1956; *New York Times*, Nov. 14, 1958. For the complexities of this problem see the note "Racial Discrimination in Housing," *University of Pennsylvania Law Review*, 107: 515–550 (Feb., 1959); *Where Shall We Live? Report of the Commission on Race and Housing* (Berkeley, 1958).

complaints were settled before the Committee was killed by congressional action in 1945. But, by and large, until 1951 the antidiscrimination clause was "little more than an expression of pious hope." Since that time, however, this program of reform in civil rights has, under the aegis of the presidency, met with some success.[63]

President Truman revived the program in 1951 by setting up the Committee on Government Contract Compliance over the opposition of Southern Democrats and some congressional Republicans.[64] The Committee possessed limited powers to investigate violations of nondiscrimination clauses and could "confer and advise" with firms in order to bring about compliance. Committee recommendations were submitted to the Director of Defense Mobilization who had direct access to the President. The limited staff, funds, and powers of the Committee together with the current bogey of FEPC in Congress restricted its effectiveness.

With a change of administrations a new Committee on Government Contracts was established by President Eisenhower in August, 1953.[65] In the first phase of its operations, what is properly called "the Nixon Committee" developed an elaborate procedure for processing complaints through the contracting agency and ultimately through the Committee

[63] Robert S. Pasley, "The Non-discrimination Clause in Government Contracts," *Virginia Law Review*, 43: 837 (1957). See also John F. Cushman, "Mediation and Education for Equal Economic Opportunity," in Milton R. Konvitz and Clinton Rossiter, eds., *Aspects of Liberty* (Ithaca, 1958).

[64] Executive Order 10308, Dec. 15, 1951.

[65] Executive Order 10479, strengthened by Executive Order 10557 which extended nondiscrimination beyond hiring to promotion, transfer, etc. See Pasley, "The Non-discrimination Clause," and Cushman, "Equal Economic Opportunity," *passim*.

itself and instituted a program of publicity and education within industry. The Committee seldom intervened directly with firms which were laggard in meeting the contract standards of nondiscrimination but relied rather on less forceful means of persuasion. In the second phase, following the appointment of a new executive administrator to the Committee, the operations were invigorated by direct contacts with many of the firms still practicing discrimination in their hiring and promotion policies.[66] The power to terminate contracts in the face of discrimination was not used by the Eisenhower committee, although on occasion threats to withhold contracts or the right to bid on government contracts brought about an improvement in discriminatory situations. The Committee was sometimes hampered by an administrative atmosphere in which conferences and publicity seemed to be preferred to direct and determined negotiations with firms holding contracts; it was also hampered by the deficiencies inherent in any committee structure and the very complexity of the problem at hand.[67] For example, although

[66] Cushman, "Equal Economic Opportunity," 124; Peters, *The Southern Temper,* 255–261. The marked change in the operation of the Committee, following the appointment of a new administrative head, is a significant example of the creative use of the President's appointing power and the necessity for administration support of programs in the civil rights field. Here the primary figure was the Vice-President, not the President. The new appointee had been Washington director of the American Civil Liberties Union, and his efforts to reduce discrimination were closely tied to the political future of the Vice-President. For the official account of the activities of the Committee, see the *Sixth Report from the Committee on Government Contracts* (1959).

[67] It is the opinion of one authority close to the operations of the Committee that its greatest weakness was its structure as a committee and its interdepartmental character. The committee structure in-

industry might be willing to hire without discrimination, labor unions, particularly of the craft variety, perpetuated racism in their own select policies. Furthermore, a lack of skilled Negro labor is partly a result of apprenticeship programs which the Committee was unable to attack directly.[68] In spite of this, modest progress has been made. The fact that the Committee was styled the President's Committee and that Vice-President Nixon as chairman gave it considerable political support increased its prestige and strengthened the executive's antidiscrimination efforts. A more vigorous program will be required in the years ahead. With a current average of six million contracts and a work force approximating fifty million involved in production for the government, contract compliance can become a particularly fitting example of how the weight of the presidency may be used to sustain civil rights.

Finally, commentary on the penetrating influence of the policies and practices of the national executive is incomplete if attention is not drawn to the impact of national administrative traits on state and local governments and on private

---

stitutionalized disagreement and exacerbated the play of political, departmental, and personal friction. A partial solution, according to this observer, would be to avoid the committee form and place this important operation under a single administrator located in the White House and directly responsible to the President (confidential interview, May 5, 1960).

[68] The executive, however, could use its power to open up apprenticeship programs by denying matching funds to state-supported apprenticeship programs which perpetuate discrimination. See Irving Kovarsky, "Racial Discrimination in Employment and the Federal Law," *Oregon Law Review*, 58: 78–80 (1958), and Herbert Hill, *The Negro Wage Earner and Apprenticeship Training Programs* (New York: NAACP, n.d.), *passim*.

groups. As for negative effects, it is necessary only to note the spread of hyperloyalty from national to state and local governments. The Attorney General's list, for example, has become the guidebook of many a local loyalty purge and has been misused in ignorance and opportunism. The personnel security program, pushed far beyond the needs of real security, has spread to private industry, and even to wrestlers in Indiana.[69] One of the most dangerous aspects of the situation in connection with the national administrative arm, then, is the infectious nature of its failures.

Other instances of Federal influence are more reassuring. They would seem to indicate that a new trend of co-operation with state and local governments, to the benefit of individual liberties, is emerging. The trend demonstrates a recognition by the Federal government that the greater number of due process of law and minority rights violations are committed at the local level and that the superior sources of information as well as certain sanctions of the Federal executive can be used in a co-operative attack on the problem. Ironically, that most suspect of all national agencies, the FBI, has established a pattern for this kind of activity. The FBI, aware of the close correlation between poor training, faulty law enforcement, and injustice, has maintained training programs since 1935 for local law enforcement officers both in Washington and at the local level. In recent years special schools on constitutional rights have been held. The Director of the FBI has stated that

[69] *Hearings before the Subcommittee on Constitutional Rights of the (Senate) Committee on the Judiciary,* 84th Cong., 2d Sess., p. 350 (1955).

the course of instruction for Special Agent training and the FBI National Academy includes lectures on civil rights, ethics in law enforcement, the Constitution and the Bill of Rights, and the laws pertaining to arrests, searches and seizures. Beginning in 1954, the FBI launched a series of special civil rights schools for law enforcement agencies and when concluded in November, 1956, a total of 533 of these schools had been held at the specific request of local, county, and state authorities.[70]

By 1952 the training programs had brought into contact with scientific police work some 2,400 local law enforcement officers who, as instructors, are said to have influenced some 100,000 others. In view of the tendency of local police, through ignorance or design, to violate due process of law and civil rights, this continuing program is of critical importance.

Another example of co-operation—and one that might well have been put to use after World War II—took place in 1940. President Roosevelt, sensitive to the threat of vigilantism as war approached, called a conference of three organizations of state executives. Two hundred and fifty representatives of the Governors' Conference, the Council of State Government, and the National Association of Attorneys General met in Washington and were reminded by both presidential letter and the Attorney General of the dangers of law enforcement by untrained, self-appointed policemen. At

[70] J. Edgar Hoover to the author, May 22, 1958. See also Hoover, "Civil Liberties in Law Enforcement," *Iowa Law Review*, 37: 185–195 (Winter, 1952); Roscoe Drummond, *New York Herald Tribune*, April 6, 8, 1956; and the remarks of Attorney General Rogers, *New York Times*, July 11, 1960.

the same time these officers were urged to leave problems involving sedition, espionage, and aliens in the hands of the Federal government. Both the Attorney General and the President were anxious to avoid the Palmerism of World War I. The Attorney General declared that the conference was invaluable: "Gradually the vigilante spirit which had been giving concern to responsible officials waned." [71] In much the same way President Truman addressed the Attorney General's Conference of Law Enforcement in 1950 and reminded the participants that prosecution of crime included an obligation to protect due process and equality before the law. It is this type of conference, with invitations to school administrators and others, which was urged on President Eisenhower following the Supreme Court desegregation decision in 1954.

Although the Federal executive has failed to use systematic co-operation as a means of offering guidance in desegregation to local communities and states, there are signs of increasing co-operation in other attacks on discrimination. In what has been called "the first instance of Federal action to implement a state civil rights law," the FHA ruled in 1957 that builders of publicly assisted housing who violate the New York State law against discrimination would be denied Federal mortgage insurance. In 1958 the Veterans Administration took the first steps in assisting the New York Commission against Discrimination by agreeing that builders discriminating on racial grounds against a veteran would face disqualification for housing loan benefits. An official policy finally evolved in

[71] Francis Biddle, "Civil Rights in a Time of Stress," *Bill of Rights Review*, 2: 16 (Fall, 1941).

which both agencies refused to do business with builders violating state or city laws against discrimination, although implementation of the policy was far from perfect.[72]

The necessity for Federal-state co-operation in the field of civil rights is made forcefully apparent by the problems of state antidiscrimination agencies. Here consultation and common action by state agencies and the President's Committee on Government Contracts are called for. By way of illustration, the State of New York may enforce the provisions of its antidiscrimination law against air lines with offices in New York only if the actual hiring is done there. If the firm attempts to avoid the law by hiring in another state, the New York law is effectively nullified unless the national government intervenes. Local commissions may attempt to end discrimination in hiring within a city only to find employers with Federal contracts moving their employment offices outside the locality. The President's Committee is not without power in these cases. The original authorization under the executive order states that the Committee may "establish and maintain cooperative relationships with agencies of state and local governments . . . to assist in achieving the purposes of this order." [73] Part of the unfinished business in civil rights is to establish positive co-operation between Federal and state agencies and to overcome the reluctance of the Federal government to withhold funds from programs which

[72] *New York Times,* June 4, 1958; *Business Week,* July 19, 1958. See also the *Report of the United States Commission on Civil Rights,* 1959, pp. 457–470.

[73] Charles Abrams, "Our Relations with Federal Agencies" (Address before the Fifth Annual Conference of Commissions against Discrimination, June 11, 1957 [mimeo.]).

sanction discrimination. The potentialities of this technique are only beginning to be explored.[74]

Conclusion

This is the record and the promise of a rich variety of administrative measures available to a President who would use his administrative powers to promote and encourage individual liberty. The past presents a pattern of misuse of these powers in many instances where security clashed with the Bill of Rights but also a positive, if unsystematic, use of the same instruments for promoting minority rights. Much will depend on the desire of the executive branch to correct the imbalance in the future and on an executive will to enliven the available instruments. The possibilities for presidential action, however, do not stop here. The appointing power, the creative use of discretion, and the various methods for administrative direction and control mix with the executive's correlative obligation to see to the faithful execution of the laws.

[74] See Ch. V.

IV

Executive Equity and Energy

IT is clearly within the authority of the President to affirm individual liberties by administrative means and to impose restraints within his own household. But he must meet, as well, the challenge of constructive choice and the use of appropriate means in seeing to the faithful execution of the laws. The underlying conditions which contribute to sound administrative practices have already been discussed. Other questions regarding the executive powers of the President deserve attention, however. They have found contemporary focus in Federal prosecutions related to subversion, in the application of the civil rights statutes, and in the use of full presidential power in Little Rock. In broad terms they encompass executive equitable choice and energy—choice and energy which will determine whether, with what authorization, and by what means the laws will be faithfully and wisely executed.

Executive Equity

Justice Holmes, commenting on the World War I "espionage" cases, wrote to Harold Laski:

I sent you yesterday some opinions in the Debs and other similar cases . . . I greatly regret having to write them . . . and (between ourselves) that the Government pressed them to a hearing. Of course I know that donkeys and knaves would represent us as concurring in the condemnation of Debs because he was a dangerous agitator. Of course, too, as far as that is concerned, he might split his guts without my interfering with him or sanctioning interference. But on the only questions before us I could not doubt about the law. The federal judges seem to me (again between ourselves) to have got hysterical about the war.[1]

The thinly disguised disdain of the Justice for this misuse of executive energy reflects one constitutionalist's view of the damaging effects of inappropriate choice in law enforcement. The World War I prosecutions did not enhance the security of the country, and in the process individual liberties suffered. The instance is not unique. Here as elsewhere the executive might have sustained both liberty and security by exercising its option *not* to prosecute. Law enforcement, in sum, is necessarily selective, and the element of selection can be utilized to favor or damage individual liberties.[2]

[1] Holmes to Laski, March 16, 1919, in Mark De Wolfe Howe, ed., *Holmes-Laski Letters* (Cambridge, 1953), 1: 190. He added, "I should think the President when he gets through with his present amusements might do some pardoning." The cases were *Schenck* v. *United States*, 249 U.S. 47 (1919), *Frohwerk* v. *United States*, 249 U.S. 204 (1919), and *Debs* v. *United States*, 249 U.S. 211 (1919)

[2] "Law enforcement is not an automatic mechanical process. It is a very human process calling for the exercise of wide discretion. A legislature swayed by a gust of hysterical public opinion may pass a law broadly repressive of free speech and press. . . . But it is the prosecutor, the district attorney, or the attorney general, who decides whether A, B, and C shall be arrested, indicted, and brought to trial for violating that statute. These executive officers may act with ruthless and efficient zeal to suppress minority opinion by a campaign

To pretend, both as a question of law and as sound public policy, that the Department of Justice possesses no such option is to obscure with a legalism ("all laws will be strictly enforced") a broad expanse of creative flexibility where individual liberties are concerned. Many factors will determine whether a case will be prosecuted. A case may be pressed to favor the political ambitions of a local district attorney or the national administration. The probability of a successful prosecution, the adequacy of evidence, or the appropriateness of an individual case in establishing a legal rule is always a consideration, as are also questions of political advantage and fears of charges of "softness" to one thing or another (in recent years usually communism). Of most significance here is the reluctance to bring a case where the damage to liberty may outweigh the dubious gains of a successful prosecution. Liberty may be served, then, by the salutary silence of the prosecuting agency; conversely, liberty may be undermined by unwarranted and self-interested zeal in prosecution.

In this respect it is instructive to compare the experience under the Wilson administration with the later years of the Roosevelt presidency.[3] Holmes's letter to Harold Laski is contemporary evidence of a record that is now well known. District attorneys, virtually uncontrolled by Washington, ran up an impressive total of unimpressive convictions. Roosevelt's Attorneys General did better. For example, Attorney

---

of witchhunting, or they may proceed with an even-tempered caution to enforce the law only in cases of its clear and flagrant violation" (Robert E. Cushman, "Civil Liberty and Public Opinion," in *Safeguarding Civil Liberty Today* [Ithaca, 1949], 91).

[3] See pp. 20–29 above.

General Jackson, despite clear statutory authorization, refrained from prosecuting American volunteers for the Spanish Civil War.[4] Attorney General Biddle always opposed those who favored shotgun prosecution under deportation and sedition acts. Such restraint requires executive officers who have the courage to stand up to the prejudices of the day as well as a disinterested awareness of the impact of prosecution on the individual, the public mind, and constitutional principles; in every instance it requires a reflex of doubt toward the demands of the police mentality and congressional sentiment. Above all, it calls for presidential attention to the appointment of Attorneys General who are sensitive to the potential injustices of a legal prosecution which is lawful but not wise. They, in turn, must control their own agency in Washington and in the field.

Here again Attorney General Biddle's performance provides a model. On his insistence, sedition cases during World War II had to be endorsed by the Department of Justice in Washington or carried out under the guidance of the highest standards of executive action. As he wrote in a directive to all United States district attorneys:

This Department will oppose any curtailment of those rights beyond that absolutely necessary to the efficient conduct of the military and the war effort of the United States. Indeed, a further disregard for civil rights can only be viewed as distinctly injurious to national morale and subversive of the democratic ideals which the nation is seeking to defend.[5]

[4] *The Secret Diary of Harold L. Ickes: The Lowering Clouds* (New York, 1954), 132.

[5] Department of Justice Circular 3356, May 21, 1940, Franklin D. Roosevelt Papers, Roosevelt Library, Hyde Park, N.Y. See also the *New York Times*, Feb. 6, 1942.

In another instance Biddle refused to apply Executive Order 9066 (which authorized the evacuation of the Japanese-Americans from the West Coast) to naturalized citizens of Italian and German descent. Despite strong words from the Secretary of War, the Attorney General held that prosecution was justified only where there was direct military danger. When he refused to prosecute for their disobedience to military exclusion orders two American citizens with a record of sympathy for fascism, Stimson appealed to the President, protesting, "The Attorney General should not be permitted to thwart the military commanders." Biddle replied to this remarkable statement by pointing out the legal deficiencies of the cases and seemed to evidence a constitutional distaste for unnecessary prosecution. As for the pretensions of the military, Biddle remarked, "We have not approved the Army procedure, which does not permit the persons excluded—American citizens—to confront witnesses before the Military Tribunal. This is against a fundamental conception of constitutional rights." [6] In brief, here, as in other instances, the government refused (to paraphrase Justice Holmes) "to press the case," and liberty benefited without a noticeable diminution of national security.

Since World War II, this type of choice has, more often than not, been lost in the rush to strictly enforce the law. For

[6] Stimson to Roosevelt, March 31, 1943; Biddle to Roosevelt, March 3, 1943, April 17, 1943; Roosevelt to Francis Biddle, April 7, 1943; all in the Roosevelt Papers, Roosevelt Library. See also the *Annual Report of the Attorney General*, 1943, p. 8: "The military authorities recommended prosecution of numerous cases of curfew violations involving both citizens and aliens, but this department declined to prosecute excusable minor violations where no conceivable danger to national security appeared." And for the exclusion orders, see *ibid.*, p. 9.

example, the government need not have pressed for the many legal but unwise deportations or for the withdrawal of a pension from a legless war veteran because of his membership in the Socialist Workers party. It need not have harassed such individuals as Owen Lattimore and Val R. Lorwin with repeated prosecution. One government attorney, when questioned about the meagerness of evidence in a perjury indictment against Lorwin (a State Department economist), indicated "that he felt it was preferable to indict Mr. Lorwin on slight evidence rather than to appear before a Senate Committee to explain why he had not obtained an indictment." [7] He was fired for his indiscretion and confession, but one suspects that his statement reflects the origin of much of the active life of the Department of Justice in these years.

Executive equity, in brief, calls for a decision not to enforce the law rigidly in cases where injustice may result. It always requires that the law be not enforced perversely. Needless to say, executive equity is justified only if it does not inhibit vigorous and fair prosecution when the threat of subversion is real or when the failure to prosecute may undermine popular confidence in the government. Perhaps, in this respect, the basic error of the Truman administration was not in prosecuting the first-string Communists (and partly with an eye to the elections of 1948) but rather in failing to prosecute at an earlier date in order to remove the excuse for extreme internal security legislation and to assure the nation that the real conspirators were under control. What appears in retrospect to have been quite unnecessary was the later prosecution of the second- and third-string Communists

[7] *New York Times,* May 26, 1954.

when the party itself was reeling and under tight FBI surveillance.[8]

Much the same distinction can be made between the justified deportation of hard-core Communists and the deportation of certain unfortunate individuals who had innocently though indiscreetly associated with the Communist party or Communist fronts. Security may demand restrictions on liberty in order to express the determination of the government to suppress real threats; justice, however, neither requires nor permits harassment. In the anti-Communist excitement after World War II, political pressures and an assortment of undistinguished Attorneys General unhappily produced just this result. The Lorwin case alone would confirm this generalization.

By 1955, signs were visible of a shift in administrative attitudes. The government, for example, showed no enthusiasm for enforcing that legislative monstrosity, the Communist Control Act. The legless war veteran finally received his pension, and the Lorwin indictment—like others where tainted testimony was involved—was quashed. Partly as a result of increased pressure from the judiciary, the Department of Justice removed various organizations from the Attorney General's list, stating that the available evidence failed

[8] The Truman administration apparently tried to be gentle with conscientious objectors and went to great lengths in some instances toward a workable executive equity. It was suggested at one time that, when conscientious objectors refused to register, United States attorneys could become "special registrars" for the objectors and register for them. As for prosecution, "Except in the most willful instances, indictments should not be brought in future cases of religious objectors who refuse to submit for registration" (circular from the Assistant to the Attorney General, May 26, 1949, Harry S. Truman Papers, Truman Library, Independence, Mo.).

"to meet the strict standards of proof" (a weakness which had failed to worry the Department before that time), and refrained from pressing other cases.[9] Whatever the legal rationale, the inclination to be less zealous seemed to be infused with a renewed sense of the damaging effects and dubious gains of this misuse of executive power.

A dramatic example of this type of constructive executive policy appeared in 1959 when the Department of Justice, speaking through Attorney General Rogers, revived the Biddle spirit in a strong assertion of the principle of executive equity. Immediately following the Supreme Court's decision affirming the power of state and national governments to prosecute an individual for the same offense in both jurisdictions without violating the constitutional prohibition against double jeopardy,[10] the Attorney General announced a self-denying ordinance for the Federal government. In a directive to all Federal district attorneys he declared that there would be no Federal prosecution following a state trial for the same act unless the reasons were compelling and only after clearance with the Attorney General himself. Rogers stated that, although the Supreme Court decision was sound law,

applied indiscriminately and with bad judgment, it, like most rules, could cause considerable hardship. Applied wisely, it is a rule that is in the public interest. . . . Those of us charged with law-enforcement responsibilities have a particular duty to act wisely and with self-restraint in this area.

[9] For examples of this see the *New York Times*, Sept. 12, 1958; *Washington Post and Times Herald*, Jan. 3, 1959.
[10] *Abbate* v. *United States*, 359 U.S. 187 (1959); *Bartkus* v. *Illinois*, 359 U.S. 121 (1959).

The Attorney General touched the essence of executive equity when he declared, "The mere existence of a power . . . does not mean that it should necessarily be exercised." [11]

Before a discussion of the execution of the law in the field of civil rights two other types of executive discretion in law enforcement deserve brief mention. One is government participation in court proceedings as *amicus curiae;* the other is the highest form of executive equity, the use of the President's pardoning power. Either on the request of a Federal court, as in the Little Rock proceedings, or on its own voluntary motion, the government may throw the weight of its legal talent and prestige to the side of individual liberties. *Amicus curiae* is adopted, and has been used, in civil rights proceedings, the most notable instances being the Hoxie, Arkansas, desegregation case and the *amicus curiae* brief submitted in the desegregation cases when they were argued before the Supreme Court. It is significant in this connection that the end of segregation in restaurants in Washington was hastened by one of the first acts of the Eisenhower administration, the appearance of the government as *amicus curiae* in the Thompson restaurant case.[12] Until legislation

[11] *New York Times,* April 6, 1959. In the same vein, see Attorney General Rogers' word of caution after *Barr* v. *Matteo,* 360 U.S. 564 (1959), *New York Times,* July 13, 1959; and note the self-restraint in *Petite* v. *United States,* 80 S. Ct. 450, where the Department of Justice withheld a double prosecution for false statements in deportation hearings in two localities.

[12] The major instance, of course, was *Brown* v. *Board of Education,* 347 U.S. 483 (1954); another noteworthy example was *Sweatt* v. *Painter,* 339 U.S. 629 (1950). See Walter White, *How Far the Promised Land* (New York, 1956), 182; for the appearance of a Department of Justice brief before the Interstate Commerce Commission opposing discrimination in interstate transportation, see

is passed permitting the Department of Justice to intervene directly to bring about desegregation in the schools in the South—and the prospect for passage is a dim one—the *amicus curiae* weapon will be an important one as a secondary mode of executive intervention.

Whereas *amicus curiae* can be applied only with the concurrence of the Federal courts, the pardoning power is an independent presidential act. Hamilton recognized its significance in *Federalist* 74 when he remarked, "The criminal code of every country partakes so much of necessary severity, that without an easy access to exceptions in favor of unfortunate guilt, justice would wear a countenance too sanguinary and cruel." Because it is an extraordinary act open to political criticism and charges of favoritism, the pardoning power must be used with restraint. Its use is limited, too, by the President's obligation to uphold the judicial process and the legitimate requirements of security. But in law there are few limits to the use of the pardoning power.[13] Although there is some doubt concerning the Presi-

---

Attorney General Brownell's testimony, *Hearings before a Subcommittee of the (House) Committee on the Judiciary*, 85th Cong., 1st Sess., "Civil Rights," p. 576 (1957). Commenting on *Shelley* v. *Kraemer*, 334 U.S. 1 (1948), in which the Supreme Court removed the legal underpinnings of restrictive covenants, one authority has said: "Without the Government's intervention [as *amicus curiae*] it is doubtful if the Supreme Court would have accepted review" (Charles Abrams, *Forbidden Neighbors: A Study of Prejudice in Housing* [New York, 1955], 220).

[13] Edward S. Corwin, *The President: Office and Powers* (New York, 1957), 158–169; Everett S. Brown, "The Restoration of Civil and Political Rights by Presidential Pardon," *American Political Science Review*, 34: 295–300 (April, 1940); W. H. Humbert, *The Pardoning Power of the President* (Washington, 1941).

dent's power to pardon for contempt of Congress (a use of the weapon which might have become significant if the curve of congressional irresponsibility had continued to rise after 1954), there seems to be no constitutional restraint on the power of the President to pardon all individuals convicted under Federal statutes.

On occasion, consequently, the pardoning power can be a fruitful means of presidential protection of individual liberty. It may be used, for example, as a symbolic act of presidential opposition to sentiments which have swept the judiciary and the public. Beyond the argument of individual mercy and despite compelling reasons to the contrary, the Eisenhower administration might have encouraged a charitable national climate by commuting the sentences of the Rosenbergs or their lesser confederates.[14] The pardoning power actually has been used to block deportation which would have taken place automatically after the completion of a sentence for certain offenses committed by aliens against the United States.[15] In addition, it should be noted that this presidential prerogative is one of the few executive acts which can re-create civil rights, lost whether rightly or wrongly by conviction for a crime. As one state court explained:

A man may be convicted wrongfully. Good men sometimes commit crimes or misdemeanors. Provocation and passion are liable to occur to all, and under their sway the best citizen might subject himself to conviction for what the law denominates a crime or misdemeanor. His guilt may be technical. There may be much

[14] Robert J. Donovan, *Eisenhower: The Inside Story* (New York, 1956), 45–50.
[15] Corwin, *The President,* 415.

to extenuate his act [or belief, if one considers past membership in the Communist party] in obedience to the promptings of passion under severe trial from provocation. He may have universal sympathy from his fellow citizens, who have known how well he discharged his duties in life, and who make allowance for his act, but the law demands and secures his conviction. . . . Henceforth this citizen is excluded from the suffrage, while thousands less worthy are allowed to exercise the right of suffrage simply because it may be that justice has not overtaken them. A frame of government which tolerates such a result would be seriously defective.[16]

Finally, the President's pardoning power can be used to atone for and repair the unfortunate results of convictions in earlier periods of governmental and public excess. Woodrow Wilson refused to pardon Eugene Debs and others for their "crimes" under the Espionage Act. The challenge was met with more charity, however, by President Harding, who pardoned Debs and in other cases commuted the sentences to the time already served. Again, in 1933, President Roosevelt in a Christmas amnesty restored civil rights to fifteen hundred victims of the World War I prosecutions.[17] The tradition, we should remind ourselves, extends back to the Jeffersonian presidency after another notable period of irresponsibility within the Federal government. In a letter to the wife of the foremost proponent of the Sedition Act of 1798 Jefferson defended his use of the pardoning power:

[16] *Jones* v. *Board of Registrars,* 56 Miss. 766 (1879), quoted in Brown, "The Restoration of Civil and Political Rights," 297.

[17] *New York Times,* Dec. 25, 1933; Humbert, *The Pardoning Power,* 94. For President Roosevelt's pardon of Earl Browder see Zechariah Chafee, *Blessings of Liberty* (Philadelphia, 1956), 28–29.

I discharged every person under punishment or prosecution under the sedition law, because I considered, and now consider, that law to be a nullity, as absolute and palpable as if Congress had ordered us to fall down and worship a golden image; and that it was as much my duty to arrest its execution in every stage, as it would have been to have rescued from the fiery furnace those who should have been cast into it for refusing to worship their image. It was accordingly done in every instance, without asking what the offenders had done, or against whom they had offended.[18]

The pardoning power is an exceptional instrument and restorative rather than preventive. As the highest form of executive equity it repairs after the fact; the deeper responses of executive equity, on the other hand, attempt to avoid the error or the excess in the first instance. In each case, however, the spirit of executive equity is the same: an independent executive decision lifts the weight of literal and rigid enforcement from the individual in cases where liberty will be harmed and where security or the integrity of law enforcement will not be seriously threatened.

Enforcement of the Civil Rights Statutes

Executive selectivity has its creative place in the enforcement of the civil rights statutes as it does elsewhere. It would be difficult to justify the prosecution of a state or local official in the presence of his serious but yet unsuccessful efforts to meet the requirements of Federal law. Nevertheless, the needs of the present day in civil rights are to quicken a retarded pace in enforcement, not to control an

[18] Jefferson to Abigail Adams, July 22, 1804, *Works of Thomas Jefferson* (Ford ed.; New York, 1905), 10: 87–88.

immoderate national tempo. For this reason alone presidential responsibility is to see to vigorous enforcement of the few laws available to protect civil rights.

There is a growing amount of legislative authority for presidential action, even though the statutory accumulation continues to be well restricted by involuted procedures and statutory nods of respect to the states or localities. Most momentous, of course, was the passage of the Civil Rights Acts of 1957 and 1960.[19]

For much of the period between Reconstruction and the passage of this legislation the Department of Justice was hampered by barriers of vagueness within the statutes themselves and a lack of enthusiasm for enforcement on the part of all branches of the Federal government. Executive timidity was reinforced by congressional indifference and the Supreme Court's narrow interpretation of the statutes. Above all, enforcement was dependent on the co-operation of local police officers and white juries, neither as a rule friendly to an invasion of the South by Federal law and prosecution in defense of the rights of Negroes.[20] Apart from the latest voting statutes, the law as it stands today permits the Federal government to bring a suit where there is a violation of a Federal right under "color of the law" and where two or more persons conspire to deny a citizen his rights.[21] Further,

[19] For the legislative history of these statutes see Ch. II.

[20] See Robert K. Carr, *Federal Protection of Civil Rights: Quest for a Sword* (Ithaca, 1947), chs. iii–vi, for a discussion of enforcement problems under these early civil rights statutes.

[21] These guarantees appear in Sections 241 and 242 of Title 18 U.S.C. The Court, speaking in *United States* v. *Classic*, 313 U.S. 299, 326 (1941), defined "color of the law" thus: "Misuse of power.

again where a Federal right is involved, private civil suits may be brought for damages incurred by the denial of the right.

Most of the forays by the Department of Justice to protect Negro rights were beaten back by the Supreme Court and local loyalties. In order to evaluate the usefulness of these statutes, Attorney General Frank Murphy, in a notable advance for that time, established a Civil Rights Section in the Department of Justice in 1939. Murphy's experience, despite occasional successful cases, gave clear indication that new legislation would be required if the executive was to take a positive role in the protection of Federal rights. The need for legislation was emphasized by the President's Committee on Civil Rights in 1947; [22] that need was particularly obvious after the decisions in *Screws* v. *United States*

---

possessed by virtue of state law and made possible only because the wrongdoer is clothed with the authority of state law, is action taken 'under color of' state law." Presumably all rights protected against state action by the Fourteenth Amendment could be guaranteed against state infringement under the most favorable circumstances for prosecution in Section 242; but in any event, the matter is complicated because the Supreme Court has interpreted this statute narrowly, that is, a violation must be willful with "a specific intent to deprive a person of a Federal right" (*Screws* v. *United States,* 325 U.S. 91 [1945]). The conspiracy section (241) is severely limited in protecting an individual against private action; it guarantees little more than the right to inform Federal officers of the commission of a Federal crime, the right to make entries under the homestead laws, the right of access to Federal courts, the right to protection when testifying before a Federal tribunal, and, more important, the right to participate in a Federal election.

[22] *To Secure These Rights: The Report of the President's Committee on Civil Rights* (Washington, 1947).

and *Williams* v. *United States* were handed down by the Supreme Court.[23]

There is still some life in the pre-1957 statutes in clear cases of willful violation by state officials of a limited list of Federal rights. Congress has not seen fit to reshape this Reconstruction legislation but instead has concentrated on Federal protection of voting rights. Before the Civil Rights Acts of 1957 and 1960 are discussed, it should be made clear that the successful techniques of law enforcement do not always require a conviction. Although prosecution under the Reconstruction statutes has not always ended in conviction, the educational effect of the presence of the Federal government as a defender of equal rights must not be minimized. Supposedly "ineffectual" executive action is probably in part responsible for the lessening of violence by local police in the South through the 1940's. As a United States attorney remarked to the Attorney General:

The defendants are at liberty, but it is my humble opinion that the prosecution will do good for years to come. None of these state officers likes to be hauled into the Federal Court. Of course, I do not think any man should be indicted unless he is guilty; but such prosecutions as this do a lot of good in the case of a guilty defendant even though he is not convicted. It will also have its effect on other State officers.

Or in another instance:

I think the prosecution in Mississippi was beneficial. For a period of five years, no prisoner has been taken from an officer in Mississippi and lynched. The trial of the case impressed officers from

[23] 325 U.S. 91 (1945); 341 U.S. 70 (1951). See footnote 20, above.

146

the Governor down to the Constables with the importance of an officer according to a prisoner the highest degree of protection.[24]

Equally apparent is the effect of FBI co-operation with state and local authorities following acts of bombing, arson, or lynching in the South. In the same way, arrest and subsequent prosecution for a threat of violent resistance to a Federal court order may fall afoul of the prejudices of a local jury, but the violent act itself will have been deflected and the Federal presence felt.[25] Investigation or vigorous prosecution by Federal authorities, although it may cause local resentment, reminds those who condone this type of infringement of individual rights that the violation goes against the grain of the national conscience. A conviction, desirable as it may be, is not necessary to produce this effect. The same rule of indirect influence applies to the Civil Rights Acts of 1957 and 1960 in spite of their severe shortcomings.

These statutes introduced unusual legal techniques for the protection of the right to vote.[26] Either the Department

[24] To Secure These Rights, 128–129.

[25] Robert G. Dixon, Jr., "Civil Rights: Recent Variations on a Theme of Moderation," George Washington Law Review, 27: 555 (1959).

[26] The procedures under the Civil Rights Act of 1957 were tied to a civil suit against "any person [who] has engaged . . . or is about to engage in any act or practice which would deprive any other person" of the right to vote. The civil proceeding was designed to avoid a prejudiced jury trial and authorizes the court to force compliance under its contempt power. Under the Act the refusal of a local official to comply could lead to criminal contempt proceedings without a jury trial—unless the sentence is imprisonment in excess of forty-five days or the fine is over $300. The distinction between civil and criminal contempt was a major issue in the

147

of Justice or individuals who believe that they have been denied the right to vote may file complaints and bring a civil suit in a Federal District Court for an injunction against state or local authorities. After a full trial (without a jury), and if the court determines that there has been a deprivation of the right to vote because of race or color, the Attorney General may request that the court make a finding as to whether the deprivation is part of a "pattern" of discrimination. If the court so finds, after all parties are heard on the issue, it may appoint voting referees (who are themselves registered voters and residents of the judicial district) to receive voting applications from Negroes living in the voting district. The would-be voter must then try to register once again with the local registration official and, if he is turned down once more, he may register with the referee in an ex parte hearing, as long as he is qualified to vote under state law. Exceptions to the referee's findings may be filed by local officials before the court issues an order naming the

---

debate on the bill. Civil contempt is generally used by a judge to force compliance with a court order. The defendant is free of contempt when he has complied with the order. He "has the keys to the prison in his pocket." Criminal contempt is used to punish the commission of an irrevocable act or an affront to the court; it results in a jail term for a specific period of time. The Civil Rights Act of 1960 augmented these procedures by adding "referee" and hearing provisions. Two other significant additions authorize the Department of Justice to sue a state in the event of resignation or other absence of local registrars (which had occurred in the Terrell County, Georgia, case) and require state election officials to preserve their voting records for twenty-two months while making them available for Federal inspection. See the *New York Times,* April 22, 1960, and *United States* v. *Raines,* 80 S. Ct. 519 (1960).

individuals who have been found qualified to vote.[27] The refusal of officials to obey the order constitutes contempt of court.

What is striking about this parade of officials and lawyers is its essential localism, the labyrinthine procedures required to assure the exercise of a right long since authorized under the Fifteenth Amendment, and the ingenious administration—as well as the intestinal and financial fortitude on the part of Negro citizens—which will be necessary if the statute is to be at all effective. The one major executive problem, consequently, is to attempt to administer a statue which shows all the signs of legislative compromise and has the mark of Southern legislative skill upon it. It should be noted that the Department of Justice has been hampered also by political and administrative realities and certain administrative presuppositions.

The administrative realities are tied to the statute as well as a strong strain of localism in law enforcement in the United States. Under the voting statutes local officials are very much a part of the proceedings, and the requirement of finding "a pattern of discrimination" places the burden on the potential Negro voter. Further, Federal judges must fight against their own local sentiments (as must the referees) while Federal district attorneys will have friends and political futures, both of which may be harmed by their responsibility to prosecute local officials. One recurrent prob-

[27] There is allowance under the Act for provisional voting where application is made twenty days or more prior to the election. The vote is subject to challenge and determination of validity after the election.

lem has been the reluctance of the FBI to investigate anything but specific complaints. The Bureau, quite properly, is averse to "fishing expeditions" but also is interested in guarding its relationship with appropriations committees in Congress and its broader responsibility for criminal investigation. The latter consideration makes the Bureau hesitant to damage associations with local sheriffs and other law enforcement officials in the states. Above and beyond these factors is the fear of economic and physical reprisal against those who do appeal to the law. It tends to reduce the number of complainants and witnesses just as it may reduce the impact of a case effectively prosecuted.

Most of these administrative realities are subject to change once given vigorous enforcement of the law and the passage of time. Even more amenable to change are two administrative presuppositions which now and then have hampered the Department of Justice in protecting Negro rights. First, the Department has been disposed to share the guardianship over federally guaranteed rights with the same state governments which seem incapable or unwilling to protect them. Instead of asserting the full and clear responsibility of the national government, when it is quite evident that the states will not bring their full power to bear in favor of constitutional rights, there has been an administrative tendency to lean far backward to give the state and local governments "a chance." This administrative psychology was evident in one nonvoting case, the Mack Charles Parker lynch-murder in Poplarville, Mississippi, when the Attorney General chose to hand the case over to the state, after stating that there seemed to be no Federal power to act. Following a foregone acquittal by a local jury he then stepped in with a Federal prosecution, long after the proper moment had passed.

The same administrative attitude was evident in the ease with which the administration permitted the introduction of local power into the Civil Rights Act of 1960. The second governing presupposition is the understandable interest within the Department in winning cases and establishing favorable interpretations of the civil rights statutes by the Federal courts. This legal psychology is questioned by those who believe that a number of cases prosecuted vigorously may be more effective than a single case won. The distinction here is between legal perfection and the deterrent effect of a number of Federal prosecutions. The glacierlike administration of the Civil Rights Act of 1957 can be criticized on this ground; but perhaps more significant was the excessive caution, redoubled by political considerations and deference to Congress, which delayed the prosecution of the first case for almost two years and limited the number of actions to a paltry few. The record of the Department of Justice led the Civil Rights Commission to conclude that "its legal actions were disappointing in number, nature, and results." [28]

In an area so sensitive to conflicting political and ad-

[28] Only four cases were prosecuted in the first three years after the passage of the Civil Rights Act of 1957: Terrell County, Georgia; Macon County, Alabama; Washington Parish, Louisiana; and Fayette County, Tennessee. By the count of the Civil Rights Commission of thirty-two cases pending in 1958 in the Civil Rights Division only seven were truly civil rights cases, three cases pertaining to voting and four "racial" cases (*Report*, 1959, pp. 131–132). The difficulty in obtaining voting records from recalcitrant local officials and certain unsettled legal questions (see *United States* v. *Raines,* 80 S. Ct. 519 [1960]) only partly explain this inactivity.

ministrative interests it seems mandatory that the President should keep a watchful eye on the administration of these statutes. He may jog reluctant administrators while lending the administrative prestige of the White House to those departments or divisions which want to act. Otherwise, the statutory insufficiencies may be compounded by administrative insufficiencies. A shift in the presuppositions mentioned above together with determined execution of the voting right statutes of 1957 and 1960 should make it possible to get blood even from these procedural stones. Such a shift seemed to be appearing in the late hours of the Eisenhower administration.[29]

The Ultimate Weapon in Little Rock

There are occasions when the execution of the laws cannot be confined to routine administration. So it was when the problem of relocating Japanese-Americans arose in 1942 and when the President initiated a crash program in the loyalty-security field. So it was, too, in Little Rock. This event was so unexpected that the same President who in July said that

[29] Immediately after the President signed the Civil Rights Act of 1960, the Department of Justice began the inspection of voting records in four Southern counties (McCormick County, South Carolina; East Carroll Parish, Louisiana; Webster County, Georgia; and Wilcox County, Alabama) where more than half the population is Negro and where no Negroes are registered to vote. Besides this vigor on the first working day after the bill was signed and subsequent moves to protect would-be Negro voters against economic reprisal, there was the possibility that the Department might use other techniques, for instance, the investigation of conditions by field representatives, in place of waiting for specific complaints, and the stepped-up utilization of trial attorneys from Washington. See Attorney General Rogers' statement in the *New York Times*, July 11, 1960, and *ibid.*, Sept. 14, 1960.

troops would be used to enforce desegregation in the schools only "over my dead body" in September dispatched troops to the South. In Little Rock the President took the long final step in fulfilling his obligation to law enforcement and the protection of liberty under the Fourteenth Amendment. The wisdom of this extreme measure will be the subject of debate for some years to come. Despite several Southern arguments to the contrary, however, the legality of the President's action is beyond question.

It is true that only in the Reconstruction period and in a few other isolated instances has the authority to use troops been used to protect civil rights.[30] But Presidents have dispatched troops on many occasions, with or without the request of a state governor or a Federal court, to suppress opposition to the law or defiance of court orders or to keep the peace. In the earliest days of the Republic, President Washington sent troops to suppress the Whisky Rebellion and even dramatized his determination to see the laws upheld by accompanying them on their way. When the supremacy of Federal law was threatened by the South Carolina Nullifiers, Jackson combined the threat of military action with political persuasion to settle the issue. With austere emphasis the President warned those who were about to defy the laws of the Union that his oath required him to resist with all the power at his command a doctrine

incompatible with the existence of the Union, contradicted expressly by the letter of the Constitution, unauthorized by its spirit, inconsistent with every principle on which it was founded, and destructive of the great object for which it was formed.

[30] For presidential use of troops see Bennett M. Rich, *The President and Civil Disorder* (Washington, 1941), *passim*.

Less sternly he added:

Let me not only admonish you, as the First Magistrate of our common country, not to incur the penalty of its laws, but use the influence that a father would over his children whom he saw rushing to certain ruin. In that paternal language, with that paternal feeling, let me tell you, my countrymen, that you are deluded by men who are either deceived themselves or wish to deceive you.[31]

The subtle mixture of presidential conciliation and firmness together with the threat to use troops shattered the Nullifiers' cause until it re-formed for the holocaust of the Civil War.

The dispatch of troops by Presidents in the post-Civil War period was usually either in response to the requests of governors for aid in suppressing industrial violence or spontaneously to enforce Federal law and protect Federal interests. President Cleveland used troops to support a court injunction against the Pullman strikers and to protect the mails. Wilson dispatched troops to prevent violence associated with strikes. President Hoover used troops to drive the bonus marchers out of Washington; this operation numbered among its personnel the then Major Eisenhower. Thus, by 1957 the use of troops to preserve the peace and enforce the law was strange neither to the President nor to the presidency.

If President Eisenhower acted within the traditions of the presidency when he dispatched elements of the 101st Airborne Division to Little Rock, the Governor of Arkansas, Orval Faubus, was not without precedents of his own. In at least four

[31] Proclamation on Nullification, in James D. Richardson, ed., *The Messages and Papers of the Presidents, 1789–1897* (Washington, 1899), 2: 643, 652.

instances since 1930 governors have called out the National Guard to defy the Federal government.[32] Fortunately, in one of these instances the Supreme Court met the challenge directly. When Governor Sterling dispatched the National Guard to prevent the execution of a court order temporarily ending controls on the production of Texas oil, the Supreme Court spoke on two important points. The Court held that the legitimacy of a governor's use of troops is open to judicial inquiry and that where a Federal right is involved the protection of that right must prevail. A unanimous Court condemned the Governor for his failure to uphold a Federal right. "Instead of affording them protection in the lawful exercise of their rights," wrote Chief Justice Hughes, "he sought, by his executive orders, to make that exercise impossible." [33] These words were particularly appropriate for the later law enforcement crisis in Little Rock.

If, in an episode so complicated, primary responsibility can be assigned, it must fall on the Governor of the State of Arkansas. Three years of constructive labor on the part of the Little Rock School Board toppled when Governor Faubus called out the National Guard to "maintain order" and pro-

[32] In 1934 the Governor of Arizona used the National Guard to prohibit a construction firm from continuing work on Parker Dam; in 1938 the Governor of Iowa called out the National Guard to stop NLRB hearings; and in 1940 Governor Phillips of Oklahoma, protesting against unsatisfactory reimbursements for the flooding of state roads, halted construction on the Grand River Dam by using the National Guard (Frederick B. Wiener, *Washington Post and Times Herald*, Sept. 5, 1957).

[33] *Sterling* v. *Constantin*, 287 U.S. 378, 402 (1932). This statement was echoed in *Cooper* v. *Aaron*, 358 U.S. 1, 18 (1958): "No state legislator or executive or judicial officer can war against the Constitution without violating his undertaking to support it."

hibit Negro children from entering Central High School on September 2, 1957. This defiance of the enforcement of Federal law and the subsequent indirect defiance when the forces of the state were *not* used to protect the Negro children in the exercise of a Federal right, if persisted in, made presidential intervention of some kind inevitable. The Governor's argument that troops were needed to preserve the peace against incipient racial violence is not evident in the record, nor was it accepted by the District Court. Three weeks after calling out the National Guard, the Governor, instead of enforcing rights decreed by the Federal judiciary, withdrew the troops, so that the approaches to Central High School were commanded by a mob and agitators from Arkansas and elsewhere. The District Court had this to say:

Up to this time [September 2], no crowds had gathered about Central High School and no acts of violence or threats of violence in connection with the carrying out of the plan had occurred. Nevertheless, out of an abundance of caution, the school authorities had frequently conferred with the Mayor and Chief of Police of Little Rock about taking appropriate steps by the Little Rock police to prevent any possible disturbances or acts of violence in connection with the attendance of the 9 colored students at Central High School. The Mayor considered that the Little Rock police force could adequately cope with any incidents which might arise at the opening of school. The Mayor, the Chief of Police, and the school authorities made no request to the Governor or any representative of his for State assistance in maintaining peace and order at Central High School. Neither the Governor nor any other official of the State government consulted with the Little Rock authorities about whether the Little Rock police were prepared to cope with any incidents which might arise at the school, about any need for State assistance in maintaining peace and order, or about stationing the Arkansas National Guard at Central High School.[34]

The Governor, anticipating violence, not only refused to see to the enforcement of Federal law but helped to precipitate conditions which hampered enforcement by other authorities, including, in the days to come, the President of the United States.[35]

As events unfolded, it became apparent that the President was neither prepared for nor committed to decisive Federal action in Little Rock. It is true that the Federal executive was the captive of events and the parochial sentiments of a state governor; but clearly the Federal government too was the captive of its own somnolence. Little or nothing had been done to prepare for a constitutional crisis of this sort; consequently the muddled administrative reaction in Washington quickened the logic of the extreme executive answer,

[34] As cited in *Cooper* v. *Aaron*, 358 U.S. 1, 9 (1958). For information on the crisis see Brooks Hays, *A Southern Moderate Speaks* (Chapel Hill, 1959), ch. vi; *Hearings before the (Senate) Committee on the Judiciary*, 85th Cong., 2d Sess., "Nomination of W. Wilson White" (1958); and vol. 41, no. 67, *Opinions of the Attorney General* (1957).

[35] Subsequent events not directly related to the President's role follow the same pattern of state defiance of the supreme law of the land. Disruption of the education of the 9 Negro students and 2,000 white students (Gertude Samuels, "Little Rock: More Tension than Ever," *New York Times Magazine*, March 23, 1958; *Cooper* v. *Aaron*, 358 U.S. 1, 13) produced a sympathetic hearing before Judge Lemley of the District Court prior to the opening of school in 1958. The District Court's stay of desegregation was overruled by the Court of Appeals and finally by the Supreme Court (*Cooper* v. *Aaron*, 358 U.S. 1, 5–14). The schools nonetheless remained closed until 1959. See Virgil T. Blossom, *It Has Happened Here* (New York, 1959).

the use of troops. Until the evening of September 24 the administration took what expedient measures were possible on such short notice by meeting the District Court's request for supporting briefs and by providing the investigatory experience of the FBI in order to determine the accuracy of the Governor's charge that a major disturbance would follow desegregation. The President in reply to the Governor's charge that a major disturbance would follow desegregation defended the FBI and his own constitutional function in unequivocal but not particularly specific terms:

When I became President, I took an oath to support and defend the Constitution of the United States. The only assurance I can give you is that the Federal Constitution will be upheld by me by every legal means at my command.[36]

The President and the Governor, in an effort to avoid an extreme solution, met at Newport, where the President was vacationing; but the Governor's apparent promise at this meeting not to obstruct the law of the land was followed by another unpredictable deviation from the proper constitutional course when he withdrew the National Guard and handed the environs of Central High School over to the mob.[37]

[36] *New York Times,* Sept. 6, 1957.

[37] The Governor did not have to withdraw the troops, of course. Under the Constitution, his oath, and the court injunction he had ample scope for upholding the constitutional rights involved here. The injunction read in part: "Provided that this order shall not be deemed to prevent Orval E. Faubus, as Governor of the State of Arkansas, from taking any and all action he may deem necessary or desirable for the preservation of peace and order, by means of the Arkansas National Guard, or otherwise, which does not hinder or interfere with the right of eligible Negro students to attend the Little Rock Central High School. September 20th, 1957." Governor

After issuing an ineffective proclamation ordering the mob to disperse, the President moved troops into the vacuum created by the withdrawal of the National Guard. The President made clear that he did so not to enforce desegregation but to uphold the sanctity of the Federal courts and Federal law. In an address to the nation, the President affirmed one part of the contemporary presidential responsibility to individual liberties. Recognizing that "the proper use of the powers of the Executive Branch to enforce the orders of a Federal court is limited to extraordinary circumstances," he stated emphatically that

the very basis of our individual rights and freedoms rests upon the certainty that the President and the Executive Branch of Government will support and insure the carrying out of the decisions of the Federal Courts, even, when necessary, with all the means at the President's command.[38]

The Southern response reflected deep and bitter memories of Reconstruction as well as a healthy American distaste for the use of military force. The Southern constitutional case, however, was by and large a patchwork of empty and untenable legalisms which reached their high point with the assertion that the Supreme Court decision decreeing an end to desegregation was itself unconstitutional. More compre-

---

Faubus later explained that he had been "forced" to make his promise to the President so that negotiations might continue (*New York Times*, Oct. 4, 1957). The wisdom of the Newport negotiations has been severely criticized. If we assume, as we must, that constitutional issues most often find their answers in nonconstitutional terms, the criticism seems unjustified. It increased the Governor's prestige but was an honest effort on the President's part to test the Governor's intentions.

[38] *New York Times*, Sept. 25, 1957.

hensible was the Southern complaint that the President could not interfere with the inherent right of a governor to preserve the peace in his state or intervene unless by request of the Governor or the state legislature.[39] The most complicated argument admitted that the President had once possessed the power to dispatch troops to enforce court orders but that the authority had been surrendered when Congress repealed these enforcement provisions in the process of legislating the Civil Rights Act of 1957.[40] No longer, it was said, could the President use troops for court decrees; the authority under law rested with United States marshals alone. The "laws" which the President was under oath to execute were the "laws" of Congress not the broader body of law decreed and interpreted by the judiciary.[41]

These arguments, as sincerely as they may be held, are without legal foundation and are constitutionally spurious. First, under the doctrine of *Sterling* v. *Constantin*, referred to above, the Federal courts have the power to review and place limits on a governor's use of troops to "preserve order" where a Federal function or Federal right is in question. Second, the irrefutable fact is that Governor Faubus' action did not preserve order but in the end generated defiance of the laws, and thus disorder. By using the power of the state to

[39] Article IV, sec. 4, of the Constitution and 10 U.S.C. 331 (1958) were used to support the Governor's argument.

[40] See Ch. II. The provision was 42 U.S.C. 1993 (1952).

[41] See the Senate debate on the nomination of Wilson White as Assistant Attorney General, *Congressional Record* (daily ed.), Aug. 18, 1958, pp. 16762–16765; Alfred J. Schweppe, "Enforcement of Federal Court Decrees," *American Bar Association Journal*, Feb., 1958. A case based on some of these arguments was dismissed on other grounds, 254 F. 2d 555 (*Race Relations Law Reporter*, 3: 447–451 [June, 1958]).

deny a Federal right the Governor, in concert with his administration, opposed the law of the land and seemed to misread his oath of office. Third, authority for presidential dispatch of troops to enforce an order of a Federal court is the result of a statutory accumulation dating back as far as 1792. Sections 332 and 333 of Title 10 of the United States Code (revised without Southern protest by Congress in 1956) permit the President to send troops when conditions make it impossible to enforce the laws "by the ordinary course of judicial proceedings" and when conditions exist which hinder the execution of the laws or when a state is unwilling or unable to protect a constitutional right. In every instance the President is sole judge of the need for troops.[42]

As for the argument that the term "laws" in the Constitution and the sections of the United States Code mentioned above do not include the "law" pronounced by judicial decree, it is clear that the Constitution uses the terms interchangeably and that the congressional intent when Sections 332 and 333 were legislated did not limit the enforcement power to statutes alone. It is only necessary here to cite the statement of Senator George Edmunds, who was in charge of the precursor of the present Section 333 as it journeyed through Congress in 1871. Senator Edmunds remarked that the bill would interpose

the calm force of law, through the judiciary, aided by the lawful executive power of the nation, to punish crime and uphold order . . . it proceeds to lend the strong arm of the nation to the assistance of that judiciary . . . whatever rights are secured to the people under it [the constitution] must be guaranteed to

[42] *Martin* v. *Mott,* 12 Wheat. 19 (1827).

them and made effectual for them at last through the instrumentality of the national government.

He added:

When the laws are opposed, when the courts are in danger of being unable to carry out their decrees, to arrest and punish offenders, the executive arm is to go to their assistance, is to oppose force to force, as is done in every city and county in the country every day, when the occasion for it occurs, under State laws and under national laws. . . . When force is to be opposed to the quiet progress of the law the arm of the nation is to resist force with force, is to gather up the offender and turn him over to the court of justice for trial. That is all there is to it. We are not attempting to overturn the judiciary; we are attempting to uphold it.[43]

In reply to the arguments that troops were used unlawfully because Governor Faubus had not requested national assistance it is only necessary to point out that such a request is indicated under the law only when an insurrection exists in a state against *a state,* a condition which patently did not exist in Little Rock. Yet, even in cases of insurrection the President may act independently.[44]

Finally, there is ample authority in Article II of the Constitution to assure that the supreme law of the land will never go unenforced for want of constitutional power. The Supreme Court over the years has affirmed the authority of the Presi-

---

[43] *Congressional Globe,* vol. 99, pp. 695–698. The Supreme Court itself said in *In re Neagle:* "In the view we take of the Constitution of the United States, any obligation fairly and properly inferrible from that instrument, or any duty of the marshal to be derived from the general scope of his duties under the laws of the United States, is 'a law' within the meaning of this phrase" (135 U.S. 1, 59 [1890]).

[44] See 10 U.S.C. 332, 333, 334 (1958).

162

dent to act without explicit statutory authorization to protect the processes of the Federal government. When approving the right of the chief executive to dispatch troops to protect the mails during the Pullman strike Justice Brewer declared:

The entire strength of the nation may be used to enforce in any part of the land the full and free exercise of all national powers and the security of all rights entrusted by the Constitution to its care. . . . If the emergency arises, the army of the Nation, and all its militia, are at the service of the Nation to compel obedience to its laws.[45]

Lack of statutory authorization cannot bend the President from his constitutional course. Taking precedence over the statutes are the constitutional command to the President to see to the faithful execution of the laws and his oath "to preserve, protect, and defend the Constitution." In the light of this simple interpretation of the President's duties, it was surely evident that in Little Rock the Constitution, and in particular the vital processes of the Federal courts, needed defending in September, 1957.

To speak of constitutionality, however, is not always to speak of wisdom. Although there is no question of the duty of the President when constitutional processes are put in jeopardy and no doubt concerning the President's power to dispatch troops, there were alternative courses of action in Little Rock and these must be explored at this point. It must be assumed at the outset that Governor Faubus' acts and the Supreme Court decision in 1954 helped to create a situation which called for vigorous action on the part of the na-

[45] In re Debs, 158 U.S. 564 (1895). See also In re Neagle, 135 U.S. 1, 59 (1890), and Corwin, The President, 147–152.

tional executive. Certainly the use of the 101st Airborne Division was not the sole immediate option open to the President. Some have suggested that the President as commander in chief could have used military police or a federalized Arkansas National Guard.

It is difficult to say why military police were not used; perhaps the implication, properly unacceptable to Americans, that military police rule is superior to the authority of civilian police, together with the inadequate prestige of military police, scotched any such suggestion. It is possible to surmise, further, that the Arkansas National Guard was not utilized in the first tense days of September because of possible conflicts of loyalty and the absence of training and high discipline so essential when troops deal with mobs of irate fellow citizens. Similarly, the suggestion that a broader District Court injunction reaching beyond Governor Faubus and those acting in privity with him could have been issued to catch members of the mob in a web of contempt is weakened by traditional judicial reluctance to issue blanket injunctions. Moreover, the situation in Little Rock demanded decisive action by an arm of the national government other than the judiciary.

Constitutionalism always calls for the proper mixture of caution and firmness: firmness in order to confront those who would disobey the law with evidence of the consequences, caution to permit those who would obey a sense that the choice, however unpleasant, is theirs. The use in Little Rock of military police, of the federalized Arkansas National Guard, or of a broad injunction would not have met this test. Clearly, the use of fully equipped airborne troops without first trying a less drastic alternative does not meet the test either. If it can be assumed that the public record tells the essential facts of the crisis in Little Rock, the measure most in harmony with the requirement of constitutionalism would have been the use of United States marshals and their deputies to accompany the Negro children to the school.

The Federal government has contended that the feelings among the mob at Central High School were so intense that sworn deputies would have been of questionable value even if adequate numbers could have been enlisted.[46] Because of the deep bitterness aroused in the South by the use of troops and the convenient propaganda symbol provided for segregationists by unsheathed bayonets this argument against an *attempt* to use marshals seems superficial. A lone marshal, standing against a mob, is probably not without dramatic force in the traditions of the Southwest. A marshal carries with him, too, a Federal presence sustained by the sanction of a $5,000 fine and three years in prison if he is impeded in carrying out his responsibilities or, in fact, if he is so much as touched by an obstructionist. If the interference is with a dangerous or deadly weapon, the penalty is either $10,000 or ten years or both.[47] The dangers to the Federal marshal and the children in such a situation were great, but a public

[46] *Hearings,* "Nomination of W. Wilson White," 42–73.

[47] 18 U.S.C. 111 (1958): "Whoever forcibly assaults, resists, opposes, impedes, intimidates, or interferes with any person designated in section 1114 of this title [a Federal judge, a United States attorney, any assistant United States attorney, or any United States marshal or deputy marshal, etc.] while engaged in or on account of the performance of his official duties, shall be fined not more that $5,000 or imprisoned not more than three years, or both.

"Whoever, in the commission of any such acts uses a deadly or dangerous weapon, shall be fined not more than $10,000 or imprisoned not more than ten years, or both."

announcement of the consequences of interference followed by the stern presence of a marshal and his carefully deployed deputies should, in this case, have been tried as a suitable constitutional alternative. Had the Federal marshal been obstructed, action in a Federal court would have followed immediately, and the penalty of the law, free of the sanction of bayonets, would have been felt in the personal lives of the ringleaders and the bigoted hard core. It is well to remember here the heavy sentences and the spirit of the statement by an English judge, Mr. Justice Salmon, to some of the toughs of Nottinghill, London:

Everyone, irrespective of the colour of their skins, is entitled to walk through our streets in peace, with their heads erect and free from fear. That is a right which these courts will always unfailingly uphold. As far as the law is concerned, you are entitled to think what you like, however foul your thoughts; to feel what you like, however brutal and debased your emotions; to say what you like, provided you do not infringe the rights of others or imperil the Queen's peace.

But once you translate your dark thoughts and brutal feelings into savage acts such as these, the law will be swift to punish you, the guilty, and to protect your victims.[48]

The decision by the Department of Justice to use marshals in Little Rock in 1958, in the event of a recurrence of the difficulties experienced a year earlier was, it seems, tacit recognition of an error in executive judgment in 1957.

What, then, of the charge that the Department of Justice was delinquent in failing to bring to trial later in the year the members of the mob outside Central High School? Here, on balance, the government's case is more persuasive.

[48] Quoted in *Encounter*, vol. 11, no. 6 (Dec. 1958), p. 5.

There is little doubt that the crowd was whipped up by organized agitators, most of whom did not live in Little Rock.[49] The efforts of the district attorney and the FBI to find clear evidence of a conspiracy, however, were unsuccessful. The situation in law was a difficult one for the Federal government. There was then only one Federal statute which seemed to permit prosecution for conspiracy in such an instance, that is, the Civil Rights Act of 1870. This statute provides a penalty of ten years in jail and/or a $5,000 fine for those who conspire to deprive a person of rights guaranteed under the Constitution. But to prosecute successfully under this inadequate statute the government had to have unimpeachable evidence of a conspiracy which, despite hard work by Federal investigating agencies in Little Rock, was not to be found. To lose a case or fail to get an indictment in Little Rock at that time would have left a dangerous impression of Federal impotence.[50]

Although the Department of Justice can be defended for its failure to prosecute under the available statutes and although there is no question of the constitutionality of presidential intervention with troops in Little Rock, there remains considerable doubt about the wisdom of using the ultimate executive weapon before other means are exhausted. It was

[49] *New York Times,* Dec. 8, 1957.

[50] The Civil Rights Act of 1960 corrected this deficiency by including a provision making it a crime to interfere, impede, or obstruct "the due exercise of rights or the performance of duties under any order, judgment, or decree of a court of the United States." For the shortcomings of the earlier statutes and the contempt power by the Federal judiciary see the testimony of Attorney General Rogers in the *Hearings before the Subcommittee on Constitutional Rights of the (Senate) Committee on the Judiciary,* 86th Cong., 1st Sess., pp. 186–189 (1959).

no comfort to the moderates and was a potentially dangerous precedent. The precipitous response of the Eisenhower administration to the events in Little Rock was part of the harvest of executive inactivity from the time of the Supreme Court decision ordering desegregation in 1954 to the opening of school in 1957. Executive passivity toward the molding of public opinion will be discussed at a later point; but two other aspects of the Federal government's laxity should be mentioned here.

First, there is no public evidence that the Department of Justice had prepared for contingencies similar to Little Rock in that creative interval between 1954 and 1957, even though threats of trouble appeared soon after the Supreme Court decisions in 1954. Apparently the Department was relying on the good will of Southern moderates, coupled with a few appearances in court (as in Hoxie, Arkansas, and Clinton, Tennessee) and the binding force of the oaths of state officers to enforce the Constitution. Even the immediate warnings of trouble in Little Rock, marked by the curious questioning by Governor Faubus of a high official in the Department of Justice as to the government's intentions in the event of a disturbance in Little Rock, were ignored.[51] Second, and more important, the President's "over my dead body" doctrine, expressing his resolve not to use troops in the South,[52] seemed to remove from the realm of possible Federal actions

[51] Warren Olney III, then Assistant Attorney General, says of his assistant's trip to Little Rock, "The Governor's subsequent action has given it a significance which was not appreciated by us at the time" (Address to the Conference of Barristers of the State Bar of California, Oct. 3, 1957, reprinted in the *Congressional Record* [daily ed.], March 24, 1958, p. 4532).

[52] Arthur Krock in the *New York Times*, Sept. 26, 1957.

the ultimate sanction of the law. Together with presidential statements casting doubt on the wisdom of the Supreme Court decision and desegregation by law alone, this statement invited defiance and helped to create the need for the very force which the President declared he would not use. As a consequence, the hurried preparations for action in Little Rock had the inherent deficiences of a crash operation in which the alternatives were not carefully plumbed and proper timing was ignored and in which the President's belated but quite proper indignation bred the extreme answer.

Why the President and his advisers were caught unprepared remains one of the major puzzles of the Little Rock episode. Few observers expected trouble to erupt in Little Rock. With the history of careful preparation by the School Board and apparent public acceptance of the desegregation plan the city was not an obvious danger spot. On the other hand, this does not excuse the lack of preparation for the unknown contingency or for trouble anywhere; trouble of some sort was clearly indicated by the magnitude of the social problems of desegregation. It must be assumed that the President was unprepared either because of the failure of his advisers to alert him to the seriousness of the problem or because of his own immersion in other affairs of state. The President's states' rights sentiments and his own self-denying view of presidential power, as well as his distaste for the use of Federal power to change social habits, would, in the first instance, have made him reluctant to plan for actions that he believed to be constitutionally unacceptable. The issues, consequently, shaped themselves, and the President was forced to impose an extreme, if only temporary, solution.

Too late, perhaps, to close the wounds in Little Rock, a

shift toward a more positive view of executive responsibility began to appear in 1958. There were still signs of the old cluster of attitudes: in the refusal of the executive branch to use contingency funds to assist in the rebuilding of the bombed-out school in Clinton, Tennessee and in the President's new "go slow" doctrine on integration and his unwillingness to endorse the morality of the Supreme Court decision. But the Department of Justice, under Attorney General Rogers, introduced a type of planning which had been absent the year before. There was no thought of using troops in the event of trouble in 1958 even though the President, quite wisely, made it clear that troops would be sent to any part of the South if court processes could not be defended by other means.[53] Instead, marshals were deputized and sent to Washington for training in police work and riot control, briefs were prepared in anticipation of action in the courts, and officials in the Department of Justice were delegated to study and keep in touch with happenings in Virginia and Little Rock.[54] The Department was careful under the new program to obtain accurate intelligence from the South while, at the same time, making certain that the point of view and the intentions of the Federal government were given publicity. Of the utmost importance were the belated efforts of the Attorney General, the President, and other public officials to sustain the dignity and constitutional function of the Supreme Court. However uncertain the President's view on the wisdom of the Supreme Court decision,

[53] The President's press conference, *ibid.*, May 15, 1958, Aug. 28, 1958; John Osborne, "Strategist-in-Chief for Desegregation," *Life*, Nov. 10, 1958, pp. 123–124.

[54] Osborne, "Strategist-in-Chief for Desegregation," 123–124; James Reston in the *New York Times*, Sept. 11, 1958.

the shift in strategy indicated that at least some of the lessons of Little Rock were not lost.

Conclusion

The administrative role in protecting and promoting individual liberties is essentially a quest for the appropriate blend of four elusive elements of executive power: affirmation, restraint, equity, and energy. Wise and persistent use of the instruments of the presidency—the appointing power, the selective and vigorous use of law enforcement, and the cumulative advances by means of the imaginative application of administrative discretion, to name only a few—can nourish freedom even in the face of Cold War pressures. Executive neglect, on the other hand, may lead to the undermining of the very substance of American constitutionalism. What must be recognized today is that sustained leadership in the field must originate in White House direction, coordination, and sensitivity. Further, as the Little Rock episode made clear, the problems in this field are least effectively solved by drastic expedients imposed at the final moment. There must be anticipation of difficulties ahead and an understanding of the consequences of restrictive policies. Programs in operation must be reviewed continually, while at the same time the White House and executive agencies must be alert to individual acts of injustice. Because the major problems will find their way to the White House, to be dealt with or neglected, here in particular there should be individuals who speak of liberty rather than security and who feel committed to a positive role for the Federal executive in civil rights.

As for the President, the nominating conventions, the voters, and circumstances will bestow the personality on the office and thus determine the intensity of the President's concern with individual liberties; but whatever the sensitivity of the President himself, it is impossible today for the President to stop the flow of problems toward his desk. If he is to fulfill his constitutional obligation to protect constitutional rights, therefore, he should exercise great care in choosing those in the White House who act in his name; he should maintain for the benefit of his own subordinates and the public an appearance of rigorously high standards where liberty is concerned; and he should, above all, make careful provision that he be kept informed.

Unfortunately there is no permanently reliable administrative scheme which can provide for orderly White House consideration of complex and diverse individual liberty problems when they arise. It is too hopeful to assume that there could be an effective central agency within the Executive Office of the President designed to receive complaints and information, to plan, or to co-ordinate presidential responsibility in this field. These problems cannot be treated in isolation from other questions of presidential policy, especially foreign relations and party politics. Further, when such issues reach the crisis stage, as they did in Little Rock, they will not be contained by an organizational formula but will seek instead the highest level of policy making. Neither administrators nor groups interested in individual liberties will force themselves to follow the predetermined path of an organizational chart. They will bypass what is ineffectual, and such a central office would probably be just that.

What is more important than any formal addition to the Executive Office is the diffuse attachment to the settled principles of constitutional liberty among the White House staff as a whole, but in particular in the counsel to the President, his appointments secretary, his press secretary, and, of course, the Assistant to the President. These officials carry a heavy obligation to constitutional rights. In addition, all recent administrations have included individuals who, by accident or design, have taken on a special responsibility for individual liberties. The presence of such individuals, their own sources of information supplemented by presidential studies and by close contact with the press and private groups, can keep the President from being trapped by the "official," self-serving fact and opinion of his own agencies. Such sensitive aides can raise questions in the early stages of policy making and introduce a counterattitude to mere security-mindedness when they speak in the President's name. Above all, they can inform him and quicken his indignation by their own candor while opening the side door of the presidential office to respected private individuals who see a spectrum of value broader than security itself. In sum, the men around a busy President have a critical constitutional role. They must educate him. Once educated, the President must, in turn, educate.

V

Public Opinion and Persuasion

IN the midst of Senator McCarthy's attack on the United States Information Agency, President Eisenhower warned the graduating class at Dartmouth College:

Don't join the book burners. Don't think you are going to conceal faults by concealing evidence that they ever existed. Don't be afraid to go in your library and read every book as long as any document does not offend our ideas of decency. That should be the only censorship.[1]

With these remarks, and the implied criticism of one of his own agencies, the President unconsciously touched upon a significant aspect of presidential responsibility. It is a dual responsibility to community opinion which calls for presidential resistance to bureaucratic restraints on the free flow of information and for presidential action to remind the nation of the enduring worth of constitutional liberty. The President may use the weight of his office against harmful attitudes whether they originate in the excesses of security-mindedness, professional loyalism, or racial bigotry, whether

[1] *New York Times,* June 15, 1953. For the President's second thoughts on this vigorous statement see his press conference, *ibid.,* June 18, 1953.

they are governmental or private. All other presidential efforts to protect constitutional rights—legislative leadership, the use of administrative instruments, and the enforcement of the laws—may wither if the American publics are not free to gather the substance of fact and opinion or are not alerted to the values at stake when constitutional guarantees are threatened. The President may speak for these values and revitalize them; he can, similarly, strive to reduce and restrain those practices in his administration which may choke off the free flow of information from which public opinion is formed.

The Nature of Government Secrecy

The need for a firm presidential hand in administration and a purposeful voice in the community is intensified by the ever-quickening crisis in desegregation and the growth of restrictive information policies which real or imagined security requirements have produced since World War II. The headlong rush to restrict information is evident in a decade's accumulation of loyalty-security programs, passport and visa restrictions, and the legal angularities of post-office censorship. Above all, it is reflected in the protective insularity of the secrecy policies of the executive branch. Since World War II, in particular, the executive branch has become a storehouse of hidden fact. Exploiting the legitimate claims of secrecy, the executive branch habitually overclassifies documents, absurdly segments scientific research, and maintains convenient shields to protect administrators from the curiosity of the public and the press.

The habits of secrecy which took hold during World War II and the administrative mythology connected with the "secret" of the atomic bomb are partly responsible for the hide-and-seek atmosphere in the Federal executive branch today. More important, however, is the vital tie between science and national security in the Cold War period. The effects of these events are compounded by the rise to respectability of the government public relations expert, whose professional interest, paralleling that of the security officer, calls for managing the news in an agency's favor. This activity is usually more palatably described as the "handling" of information to protect national security, but it usually results in stacking the deck against free democratic discussion.[2]

The authority enabling the executive branch to withhold information is found in some one hundred and seventy statutes and in constitutional reasoning which rests on the separation of powers and presidential responsibility for foreign policy.[3] Successive administrations have refused to divulge intra-administration conversations and messages on the acceptable grounds that public knowledge of policy planning in its formative stages would inhibit the free exchange of ideas within the executive branch. National security and the effective administration of foreign policy clearly justify the withholding of information dealing with departmental advice and debate, diplomatic negotiations,

[2] See Francis E. Rourke, "Secrecy in American Bureaucracy," *Political Science Quarterly,* 72: 540–564 (December, 1957). Douglass Cater in his important study, *The Fourth Branch of Government* (Boston, 1959), estimates that there are some 3,000 government "information" officers.

[3] *Report of the (House) Committee on Government Operations,* 86th Cong., 2d Sess., "Federal Statutes on the Availability of Information" (1960).

or state secrets. For these reasons, President Eisenhower refused to turn over certain information to Congress (and the public) during the Army-McCarthy hearings in 1954. As he wrote to the Secretary of Defense:

Beçause it is essential to efficient and effective administration that employees of the executive branch be in a position to be completely candid in advising with each other on official matters, and because it is not in the public interest that any of their conversations or communications or any documents or reproductions concerning such advice be disclosed, you will instruct employees of your Department that in all of their appearances before the subcommittee of the Senate Committee on Government Operations regarding the inquiry now before it they are not to testify to any such conversations or communications or to produce any such documents or reproductions. This principle must be maintained regardless of who would be benefited by such disclosures.

I direct this action so as to maintain the proper separation of powers between the executive and legislative branches of the Government in accordance with my responsibilities and duties under the Constitution. This separation is vital to preclude the exercise of arbitrary power by any branch of the Government.

By this action I am not in any way restricting the testimony of such witnesses as to what occurred regarding any matters where the communication was directly between any of the principals in the controversy within the executive branch on the one hand and a member of the subcommittee or its staff on the other.[4]

[4] Letter from the President to the Secretary of Defense, May 17, 1954, with supporting Memorandum from the Attorney General (*Hearings before the Subcommittee on Constitutional Rights of the (Senate) Committee on the Judiciary*, 85th Cong., 2d Sess., pp. 271–277 (1958).

Although the authority reaffirmed in this letter has been misused, it expressed sound constitutional doctrine. Relying on his constitutional authority, President Truman, distrustful of the irresponsibility of some segments of the American press and his own bureaucracy, issued Executive Order 10290 in 1951 establishing secrecy classifications for information in the hands of the Federal government. The President was greatly exercised by disclosures during the Korean war and, in particular, by the appearance in magazines having national circulation of data thought to be secret. After consulting with members of the press (and against their advice) the President authorized heads of all departments and agencies to classify information. The order extended to all agencies the power to impose restrictions on the release of information which had once been limited to the Departments of State and Defense and the Atomic Energy Commission. President Eisenhower attempted to meet some of the criticisms of the Democratic program in Executive Order 10501 in 1953, but with little success. In both instances exercise of constitutional power was mishandled administratively.[5]

In much the same way, authority originating in the Atomic Energy Act (and other statutes guarding the secrecy of certain crop reports, civil service forms, and tax returns) has been misused. An outstanding example of statutory distortion appeared in the administration of the so-called "housekeeping" statute which was passed in the early days of the Republic to enable department heads to make provisions for the

[5] Presidential press conference, *New York Times,* Oct. 5, 1951; Harold L. Cross, *The People's Right to Know* (New York, 1953), 206–208; James R. Wiggins, *Freedom or Secrecy* (New York, 1956), 101–102.

filing and general custody of agency records. Over the years it was transformed into a primary source of authority for the withholding of information from the public and Congress and was cited frequently by agencies to authorize secrecy. This law was amended in 1958. With the exception of this statute and certain sections of the Administrative Procedures Act of 1946 which have provided a rationale for restricting the free flow of information, all other statutes restricting information are designed either to protect the individual from unwarranted invasions of privacy, or to restrict financial speculation, or to protect national security.[6]

It should be noted that the press has every right to complain of abuses in the administration of the statutes—although one may wish that the press would be as vigorous in defense of liberties other than those which affect its own

[6] The Administrative Procedures Act (5 U.S.C. 1002) provides such broad phrases as "any function . . . requiring secrecy in public interest," matters "relating solely to the internal management of an agency," what is "required for good cause to be held confidential," and "information held confidential for good cause found" by which to enable executive officials to withhold information. The "housekeeping" statute read: "The head of each department is authorized to prescribe regulations, not inconsistent with law . . . for the custody, use, and preservation of the records, papers, and property appertaining to it." The 1958 amendment states: "This section does not authorize withholding information from the public or limiting the availability of records to the public" (5 U.S.C. 22 [1958]).

The amendment was opposed by all the major executive departments. The President, when signing the bill, attached the following proviso: "It is . . . clear from the legislative history of the bill that it is not intended to, *and indeed could not,* alter the existing power of a head of an executive department to keep appropriate information or papers confidential in the public interest. *This power in the executive branch is inherent in the* Constitution" (*Congressional Record* [daily ed.], Aug. 20, 1958; emphasis added).

179

livelihood and more circumspect in its use of some information. Congress, the press, and the public should recognize that the right to know (or the freedom of the press to acquire information) must be sacrificed on occasion for any one of a number of justifiable reasons, among them, no less than national security, the right to privacy for individuals or groups. The President must face these competing obligations and frequently protect privacy against the sensationalism so dear to the professional hearts of some members of Congress and the press. He must, of course, defend vital secrets. For these reasons President Truman issued the following memorandum to members of the executive branch when he introduced the personnel loyalty program:

The efficient and just administration of the Employee Loyalty program . . . requires that reports, records, and files relative to the program be preserved in strict confidence. This is necessary in the interest of our national security and welfare, to preserve the confidential character and sources of information furnished, and to protect Government personnel against the dissemination of unfounded or disproved allegations. It is necessary also in order to insure the fair and just disposition of loyalty cases.[7]

The solution to the problem of secrecy in government does not lie in the simple expedient of abolishing executive authority to withhold information. This will not be done and should not be done; for the withholding of information has its legitimate uses even in the service of constitutional rights, as the Truman memorandum illustrates. It is the abuse of the

[7] *Hearings before the Subcommittee on Constitutional Rights of the (Senate) Committee on the Judiciary*, 85th Cong., 2d Sess., pt. 1, p. 140 (1958).

authority which must be controlled. Failing this, scientific advance will suffer, the public will be forced to subsist on the sugar-water of the public relations man, and important aspects of public policy as well as administrative errors will go unobserved by Congress, the press, and the electorate. Unless current administrative attitudes change, it is reasonable to expect a continuation of the same heavy-handed administration which assumes that every piece of executive information is a self-contained supersecret until proved otherwise.

Government secrecy policies today have a two-way impact on freedom of information; they dry up the exchange of knowledge within the executive branch, and they inhibit the flow of information to the public. Scientists working for the government have been hampered by many barriers to the free exchange of information. For instance, the "need to know" test for access to information frequently has required a scientist working in one agency (and usually one field of research) to state his need to know before the secrets in another agency are freely available to him. The productive, though sometimes apparently aimless, discourse of wandering scientific curiosity has been constricted by a requirement which may be foreign to the inquiring mind: the ability to know specifically what one wants to know. It should be added that the "need to know" test is sometimes complicated for government scientists by the requirement for multiple clearance. This administrative device denies, except under special circumstances, access to information from and communication with colleagues working for another agency unless separate clearance for the other agency is obtained.

These examples of the restrictions on the flow of information within the government are matched by similar prohibitions on the free movement of information from the government into the community at large. One of several methods is to overclassify information by labeling it Top Secret, Secret, or otherwise, generally with a classification exceeding its true security value. It is estimated that thousands of individuals in the Federal government may and do classify data a large percentage of which does not need to be classified.[8] Moreover, because declassification requires thought and time (when classification itself requires only a single bureaucratic impulse), the amassing of additional millions of linear feet of closed files inundates the declassifiers. Whereas the act of classification involves no risk, declassification does.

The administrator who is an avid classifier is supported by the flawless logic, if not the constitutional wisdom, of riskless state security: tell the enemy nothing of scientific experimentation by the government, yield only carefully selected information concerning the background of policy formulation, for even apparently ridiculous bits of information can be put together to expose the mosaic of national defense to the enemy. One objection to this reasoning, even if it is measured by its own standard, is that overclassification actually threatens state secrecy. As the Coolidge Committee reported to the Department of Defense, overclassification was reaching "serious proportions" and was weakening the security system by its excess:

[8] Wallace Parks, "Secrecy and the Public Interest in Military Affairs," *George Washington Law Review*, 26: 36–45 (Oct., 1957); *Twenty-third Report by the (House) Committee on Government Operations*, 85th Cong., 2d Sess., pp. 32, 42 (1958).

The result is not only that the system fails to supply to the public information which its proper operation would supply, but the system has become so overloaded that proper protection of information which should be protected has suffered. The press regards the stamp of classification with feelings which vary from indifference to active contempt. Within the Department of Defense itself the mass of classified papers has inevitably resulted in a casual attitude toward classified information, at least on the part of many.[9]

Partly because, as one member of the press remarked, "The No. 1 brains of the Government draw the directives; the No. 8 brains abuse them," [10] a study of the "silent propulsion of whales" by the Woods Hole Oceanographic Institute was given a secrecy classification. In another instance, a scientific document, published in Russia, was translated and stamped secret by seven agencies of the Federal government, and the Air Force refused to release pictures of a new Red Air Force plane.[11] Similarly, although eyewitness reports of the activities of American frogmen during the evacuation of the Tachen Islands had been printed in newspapers, the Secretary of the Navy objected to the mention of this information in an article in *Collier's* magazine.[12]

In each of the instances cited above the logic of 100 per

[9] *Twenty-seventh Report by the (House) Committee on Government Operations*, 85th Cong., 2d Sess., pp. 23–24, 97–107 (1958).

[10] *Ibid.*, 147.

[11] Allen Raymond, *The People's Right to Know: A Report on News Suppression* (New York, 1955), 16; *Hearings before a Subcommittee of the (House) Committee on Government Operations*, 85th Cong., 2d Sess., pt. 14, p. 3325 (1958).

[12] *Twenty-seventh Report*, 56–57.

cent security rules: the whales presumably have something to do with the development of undersea warfare and for all the outsider knows the information once released might lead the nation's enemies to important defense secrets. The release of a picture, in turn, might reveal to the Soviet counter-intelligence sources of American information.

Another use of classification, however, defies even this system of logic. To paraphrase Secretary of Defense Charles E. Wilson, this might be called "the constructive withholding of information." In such an instance, information is withheld (sometimes legitimately) or sources of information become frozen because publication might do a disservice to the nation by disrupting the preconceived plans of American foreign policy. Thus, Secretary Wilson inaugurated (and modified under pressure) his doctrine of "constructive contribution," in administrative parlance a directive prohibiting the release of information which might reflect unfavorably on the agency or "damage" national security.[13] Constructive secrecy has produced some startling results. For example, the Office of Security Review in the Department of Defense attempted at one time to censor an article on the rearming of Franco Spain by the United States government. The *Saturday Evening Post* submitted the article, "The American Invasion of Spain," to the Department for review and accepted two deletions on security grounds. In a letter to the associate editor of the *Saturday Evening Post*, however, the Deputy Director of the Office of Security Review took issue with

[13] There was little change in substance when Secretary Wilson modified his order to permit the release of information when there was no "conflict with established policies or programs" (*ibid.*, 56).

the article's "sneering" approach. The complaint of this functionary is worth quoting at some length.

The Department of Defense and the Department of State agree that publication of the O'Donnell article in the Post would seriously react against the national security interests, at this time, of the United States. We feel there is a possibility that publication of this article would be considered offensive by Spanish authorities to the point that United States interests in Spain might be prejudiced.

. . . A few specific examples will suffice:

"Franco, that Cincinnatus with no plow to go home to * * *."

"* * * Spain was declared a pariah country by the United Nations, an outfit including such historymaking peoples as the Afghans and the Byelorussians."

"* * * the penalty for premature anticommunism curiously severe." (This comment is typical of the article, in that reference is obscure.)

"* * * second place in the Iberian League." (This would seem to be a promotion of Portugal that would be particularly galling.)

"In this corner the Americans, who believe that time is money, over against the Spanish who regard making money as a waste of time."

"For a Spanish senorita to make a decent marriage today, she has either to be born rich, win the national lottery, or latch onto a successful bullfighter."

"Some graft there may have been, since Franco's reputation for personal honesty does not extend to prominent members of his entourage."

"* * * a pastoral, donkey economy."

"* * * a country where filling stations are rarer than cathedrals * * *."

"* * * it is ludicrous to conceive, in a wartime situation, of

185

Spanish pilots mounting to ward off Soviet bombers while our jet hot rods stay back in the barracks playing canasta."

The above is just a sample. Mr. O'Donnell has not missed a single chance to insult the Spaniards in their most sensitive spots, and if occasionally accuracy is sacrificed, he seems to feel that the purpose condones this. A good example of this technique is the crack about gas stations in relation to cathedrals, which is a wild exaggeration.[14]

The ridiculous extent to which the atmosphere of constructive secrecy can go, if unchecked, is evident in an incident involving *Armor* magazine. The material in question was a book review by General U. S. Grant III, Ret., of a study of the post-Civil War period. The volume itself was published in 1879, but the editor was concerned about the constructive implications of a later day. As he explained to the Department of Defense:

In view of the fact that General Grant is a retired Army officer, I deemed it feasible to send this review in for clearance. Also, Armor is published by the United States Armor Association whose staff is comprised of one officer and three sergeants, all on active duty.

Further, due to the fact that the book is critical of the reconstruction period, which in return is critical of our Government, I deemed it advisable to protect both the reviewer and myself by having it sent through security review.

Fortunately the Department of Defense did not accept this reasoning.[15]

[14] *Ibid.*, 42–43.

[15] *Ibid.*, 45–46; for a list of generally unwarranted secrecy cases investigated by the Moss Committee, see the *Twenty-fourth Report by the (House) Committee on Government Operations*, 86th Cong., 2d Sess., pp. 4–36 (1960).

A variant of the constructive withholding of information appeared when the State Department refused to permit American newsmen to enter Communist China. Although the authority for area restrictions is soundly based, some interesting administrative attitudes appeared as the policy evolved.[16] Secretary Dulles asserted in effect that freedom of the press was the freedom to publish, not gather, the news when, in the act of gathering, American foreign policy was affected adversely. For this reason the Department of State refused to lift the area restrictions from passports of American newsmen wishing to enter Communist China and withdrew a passport from one newsman who defied the departmental policy.[17] The Secretary finally agreed to allow a selected group of correspondents to visit Communist China (although China was not granted reciprocity at first) on the condition that they stay six months and with the proviso that the passport would come up for renewal after seven months. Without much difficulty this revised policy could be interpreted as governmental withholding of access to information unless the information is handled constructively. Again, the power of the executive to withhold or interdict the sources of information is hardly debatable, but the wisdom of taking any such action was. And, as is so often the

[16] See the opinion of Judge Prettyman in the Worthy case, *Congressional Record* (daily ed.), July 2, 1959, pp. 11420–11423. The constitutional authority of the Department of State to impose area restrictions on travel was upheld in 1959. The Supreme Court denied certiorari, 80 S. Ct. 255 (1960).

[17] "Passports of Newsmen in Red China Valid Only for Return to United States," *Department of State Bulletin,* 35: 54 (1957); *Hearings before the Subcommittee on Constitutional Rights of the (Senate) Committee on the Judiciary,* 85th Cong., 1st Sess., pp. 24–33 (1957).

case where the withholding of information is concerned, the individual's right to know and national security may suffer at one and the same time. As one group of authorities concludes:

The great difficulty with area restrictions is that they are self-defeating in too many instances. It becomes a close question, too often, whether the *real* penalty is imposed upon the foreign government which is the target of the area prohibition or upon the people of this country, both those who choose to stay at home and those who desire to travel abroad.[18]

As for Communist China the policy of constructive withholding does not seem very constructive:

We have keyhole information on China. It is as if we had our eye to the keyhole beyond which there was a furnace. The revolution in China after the war is one of the most monstrous events of the twentieth century. It is an upheaval, a Himalayan upheaval, in history. We look at this revolution and these events through a keyhole. We hear a scrap from the Peking radio, and a scrap picked up by a radio in Tokyo, a clipping that manages to reach Hong Kong. Out of these fragments we try to feel our way to a meeting with this new giant of the world, which may eventually come to war with us.[19]

Presidential Counterweight to Government Secrecy

It is evident that contemporary information policies go beyond the reasonable requirements of either national se-

[18] *Freedom to Travel: Report of the Special Committee to Study Passport Procedures of the Association of the Bar of the City of New York* (New York, 1958), 54.

[19] Statement of Theodore H. White on the television program *The News from China* over WGBH-TV, Massachusetts (reprint, Fund for the Republic, 1959).

curity or the protection of confidential exchanges between administrators. An array of poorly co-ordinated programs is utilized to protect the government—and the administrator —from the embarrassment which public knowledge of error would bring; and it also tends to force from the field of public attention all but the "official" view of agency policy. Access to information and the sources of information come to be privileged, not only because of the concrete claims of national security but because of the subjection to fears of "disruption" of American foreign policy. Similarly, the classification of documents frequently follows the whim of the timid classifier's rather than a set of standards premised on the public's right to information. Timidity is intensified by the classifier's fear of the penalties for releasing the treasured secret of a given agency or for causing embarrassment to his superiors. Moreover, the administrative rewards lie with the classifier, not the declassifier. As the Coolidge Committee reported:

A subordinate may well be severely criticized by his seniors for permitting sensitive information to be released, whereas he is rarely criticized for over protecting it. There is therefore an understandable tendency to "play safe" and to classify information which should not be classified, or to assign too high a category to it.[20]

[20] *Twenty-seventh Report,* 97. See Senator Hubert Humphrey's statement on the deletion of testimony given to the Senate Subcommittee on Disarmament. The Committee reviewed the testimony before and after the executive agencies classified portions as secret. When challenged, the Department of Army restored 90 per cent of the material deleted; in another instance the Army classified testimony about maneuvers because "the Army didn't know quite what it was doing in the maneuvers"; and the CIA censored some in-

A systematic resolution of this conflict between current secrecy requirements and the citizen's need for information about his government will probably never be reached. As long as the Cold War lasts, government agencies will have unimpeachable responsibility to protect vital secrets and to give priority to national security. The authority to do so, nonetheless, inevitably will be abused, and for this reason some effective check ought to be maintained on the security officer's self-regarding sense of mission. Because the public will seldom know what it wants to know and, in turn, tends to be impressed by the myth of 100 per cent secrecy, the reassurance of Attorney General Rogers, with its reliance on public opinion, is an administrative rationalization, not a solution:

Your fears of an unwarranted withholding of information by the executive are unfounded. The true guard and judge of the reasonableness with which the executive exercises its privilege is the people, the force of public opinion.[21]

The solution lies elsewhere. Congress and the Washington press corps, in particular, have a professional interest in breaking down some of the barriers of secrecy and will, in the end, constitute the most effective counterforce. There are, however, some measures which the President can take in guarding against the excesses of his own agencies. President Truman, when he extended secrecy classification to all

---

formation because the official did not agree with the conclusions of the scientist who testified. The Department of State, with expansive editorial discretion, deleted some testimony because it was considered to be "irrelevant" (*Congressional Record* [daily ed.], June 23, 1959).

[21] *Congressional Record* (daily ed.), March 31, 1958, p. 5240.

agencies by Executive Order 10290 in 1951, announced his intention to "watch it closely" and promised that his press secretary would listen to complaints.[22] Most of his subordinates, however, seemed to remember the President's ire when he established the program, not his determination to see it administered prudently. President Eisenhower, soon after his inauguration, attempted to produce some improvements in a chaotic classification system when he issued Executive Order 10501. This order limited the power of agency heads to delegate classification responsibilities and sought a clearer definition of information which could be withheld from the public. Near the close of his second term the President withdrew the authority to classify documents from a number of agencies while denying the privilege to others without a specific grant of power.[23] In addition, a fifty-year accumulation of documents, classified before 1946, was partially declassified and the Department of Defense put a "twelve-year rule" into effect.[24] The orders, however, did not

[22] The President's press conference, *New York Times*, Oct. 5, 1951; Wiggins, *Freedom or Secrecy*, 101. The House Subcommittee on Government Information and the journalism fraternity, Sigma Delta Chi, have compiled reports citing some of the more blatant examples of unjustified executive secrecy which it would profit any President to examine. See footnote 15, above.

[23] The President did so in memoranda dated May 7, 1959, and March 9, 1960 (*Twenty-fourth Report*, pp. 164–175).

[24] Under the twelve-year rule all government documents are to be automatically open to declassification unless they are "extremely sensitive in nature." This category, open to abuse like all others, includes intelligence documents, war operations plans, and documents prepared by military commands which "concern or affect the formulation and conduct of U.S. foreign policy and plans or programs relating to international affairs" (*Washington Post and Times Herald*, July 3, 1960; *New York Times*, July 3, 1960).

dislodge the old habits. The appeals procedure was inadequate; the ridiculous number of six complaints was handled by the President's counsel in one three-year period. Restricted information, a category dropped altogether in 1953, was frequently upgraded to "confidential," and each week witnessed the appearance of a formidable stack of newly classified documents some 1,300 feet high.[25] Presidential words, without persistent oversight and a real shift in administrative attitudes, proved inadequate.

It is here that presidential weight can be felt. The White House may force certain changes in security procedures: an end to the "need to know" requirement, the introduction of common clearance for scientists in all agencies, and the establishment of a committee in the White House to accept periodically, and with an open mind, the complaints of the press concerning the unreasonable administration of classification and secrecy procedures. The President, by making his expectations known, can step up the process of declassification and reduce to the essential minimum the number of documents which fall to the stamp of the classifier.

But, in meeting this new and direct challenge to the First Amendment, nothing short of the introduction of new administrative attitudes will bring the desired change. Programmatic secrecy is alien to the American administrative experience, but, unfortunately, the early pattern of excessive concealment originating in the atomic bomb mentality of World War II and the Cold War aftermath has taken firm

[25] The estimate is made by the Moss Committee in a press release, July 24, 1960. One instance of upgrading a document to prohibit its publication concerned General Matthew Ridgway's letter of retirement. It was upgraded to "confidential" one day after it had been published in the newspapers. See the *Twenty-seventh Report*, pp. 66–67, 126.

hold. Past efforts at reform have failed because the White House has attempted to avoid a problem which its own responsibilities to national security have helped to create and because the intangible but inescapable basis of the embedded administrative attitudes—the belief that 100 per cent secrecy is desirable and attainable—has not been attacked with persistence from the highest level. The White House, somewhat paradoxically, must engage in a struggle within the executive branch, against the security tendencies of the departments and agencies which refuse to trade the convenience of secrecy for the reasonable risks which are necessary for the survival of a free society.

In brief, the President may make his presence known by periodic reminders that his agencies distinguish between secrecy and concealment. There can be inculcated, by tangible administrative rewards and respected example, an awareness of the damage to the public, the Constitution, and security itself once a pattern of excessive secrecy becomes engraved in administrative practice. A continuation of this course, for those in government and among the scientific, press, and other publics, can only result in the deadening inefficiency and threat to individual rights which is produced when the government decides on a large scale that it alone can judge what the public should know. Because there are no rules of thumb here, as in so many other areas where liberty and security meet, a favorable administrative tradition rather than a universal formula must be constructed. As one specialist in civil liberties commented before a congressional committee:

In the end . . . I do not feel that we can draw precise lines for what ought to be disclosed, and what ought not to be disclosed. We will never be able to impose fine legal controls in this area of governmental activity. Broad discretion will always be with the administrator. The safeguards, therefore, lie in attitude, tradition, and understanding.[26]

The initiation and sustaining of such a profound administrative change can come from the White House alone.

The President's Role in Public Opinion

The President's responsibility to the public in minimizing governmental secrecy is one aspect of a broader responsibility to community opinion. Beyond the President's efforts to free information from the web of bureaucratic secrecy is a profound obligation to encourage a national sentiment which is sensitive to the constitutional rights of others. At the outset it is necessary to dispense with the overly simplistic view that this obligation is fulfilled or effectively carried out by an occasional national speech or by passing references in other presidential messages. These efforts are important, particularly in times of stress or to establish a general framework for other means of presidential persuasion. But in the real world of opinion leadership there are other means of persuasion, and the principle behind them all is that a President, wishing to influence the national temper, must deal with select publics—whether they are editors, businessmen, state governors, members of Congress, religious leaders, extremists or moderates—to gain their support, or to neutralize their antagonism, for constitutional rights. They are the intermediaries, the relay stations, for the

[26] Testimony of Irving Ferman, *Hearings before a Subcommittee of the (House) Committee on Government Operations*, 85th Cong., 2d Sess., pp. 3378–3379 (1958).

presidential mood. For this reason, one small audience granted to the editors of a national magazine may be more effective than an elaborate national address. Whether in a message directed at the people or the leaders of opinion, or by other means, the President can help to build a national reflex (or a tradition) which will tend to favor equal protection of the laws, freedom of speech, and due process of law.[27] The presidential voice can be forcefully persuasive, while presidential silence can be deafening. For when the President chooses to speak publicly or deals with other leaders of opinion to instruct, inspire, persuade, or warn, he has the advantage of being the sole political figure with national identity, with singularity, and with the prestige of the historical office to sustain him.

What, under the best circumstances, may the words and actions of the President accomplish? And what values must he support and defend with the prestige and power of his office? Undoubtedly, to be at all effective, the President should make clear to the public that the internal security of the nation is protected by efficient police work and that necessary secrets are being protected, just as he should make every effort to stimulate national confidence by minimizing partisanship or mere administrative convenience in these programs. Much of the trouble over "security" in the 1950's originated in the failure of Democratic administrations to convince the nation that internal security was a matter of fundamental administrative concern; equally, the Eisenhower administration debased security by engaging in a "numbers game" over the alleged security risks dismissed

[27] See Robert E. Cushman, "Civil Liberty and Public Opinion," in *Safeguarding Civil Liberty Today* (Ithaca, 1949).

from government service. Security and individual liberty as well make up the constitutional conscience of the nation. It is a major presidential dilemma that he is obliged to protect both.

As for constitutional guarantees, the President can be an important source in reminding the nation of their existence and of their value. Because of the publicity showered on his every move the President can associate his own image with positive attitudes toward the rights of individuals. He can, by carefully directed words of advocacy, set the tone of debate when liberty is under attack. The chief executive can speak, not as a charismatic but as a constitutional leader, with quiet repetition and on occasion move dramatically to build and reaffirm popular attachment to older notions of liberty which have faced devaluation in the Cold War. In this age of veto groups and security-mindedness, his actions should show a commitment to the sanctity of the individual, to the hard core of constitutional value which manifests itself in equal protection and due process of law. He can, by the example of his own prudence, help to instruct the nation in the dangers of too much secrecy or of the suppression of the disquieting voice of the dissenter. Where the law assists minority groups, as do the civil rights statutes and many court decisions, he must make clear, without cavil or doubt, that it will be enforced. And he must be prepared in any event to accept the criticism which vigorous enforcement or his own prudence may bring. He will find that his outspoken defense of the rights of others will frequently make the popular office of the presidency momentarily unpopular.

Clearly, it is not enough for the President to reaffirm the best in the American tradition of liberty; he must fight with equal vigor the explosions of bigotry, the pressures for conformity, or disrespect for constitutional rights which are also a part of the American tradition.[28] This is his most trying responsibility, for the immediate political price may be high and the prejudice itself unreasoning. He may face at times the hostility, hysteria, or indifference of the public and its organs: the parties, Congress, and the press. A President may find himself opposed to both the confident claims of majoritarianism, of race prejudice, and of nativism and urgent administrative pleas for pragmatic short cuts through the substance of due process of law. Within this unpalatable segment of the American tradition lie violence, conformity, bigotry, and an unhealthy disrespect for constitutional restraints when they protect what in "common sense" seems to be criminal, disloyal, or out of place. Here the prestige of the presidency is especially needed—to express disdain for bigots, to explain the constitutional necessity of due process, or to support the imaginative nonconformist. When the President reminds the nation that the Fifth Amendment is not for Communists alone, that loyalty is not chauvinism, or that Negro rights are American rights his words can be a decisive public counterforce against this strain of anticonstitutionalism in the American character. He may find, too, that the pursuit of this responsibility will require him to submerge his own personal prejudices.

[28] See Samuel A. Stauffer, *Communism, Conformity, and Civil Liberties* (New York, 1955); John P. Roche, "American Liberty," in Milton R. Konvitz and Clinton Rossiter, eds. *Aspects of Freedom* (Ithaca, 1958); and an article which suggests the force of "the lone hero" in the American tradition, G. D. Wiebe, "The Army-McCarthy Hearings and the Public Conscience," *Public Opinion Quarterly*, 22: 490–502 (Winter, 1958).

It is appropriate to cite here one President's response to a newsman's question concerning the Fifth Amendment:

I personally don't want to comment on the right of a citizen to take the Fifth Amendment because I have no doubt that in some instances it is absolutely a basic safeguard of American liberty . . . although I must say I probably share the common reaction if a man has to go to the Fifth Amendment, there must be something he doesn't want to tell.[29]

The use of the term "personal" in this statement emphasizes a fact of considerable importance. A President's personal doubts about the use of the Fifth Amendment or school desegregation, for example, should not color his public statements; once they do, the doubts will be seized upon and used as an official governmental view by those who would undermine constitutional guarantees. An honest expression of his own doubts may be magnified far beyond the President's original intent. The prestige of the office is so great that, as one commentator said of President Eisenhower's wavering in the months before Little Rock, his hesitation "gave a moral base for immoral disobedience."[30] As the Little Rock crisis developed, the President seemed to recognize the corollary of this rule of presidential leadership, that is, that the efforts of the President to clarify and construct, to remind and persuade, will carry weight far greater than the mere personal views of the incumbent. He drew upon the public memory of the historical presidency when he returned from his vacation to speak from Washington about

[29] The President's press conference, *New York Times*, March 28, 1957.

[30] Charles Abrams, "New York and Little Rock" (Address before the New York Women's Bar Association, Oct. 15, 1958 [mimeo.]).

the dispatch of troops to Arkansas. "For this talk," the President told the nation, "I have come to the President's office in the White House. I could have spoken from Rhode Island, but I felt that, in speaking from the House of Lincoln, of Jackson, and of Wilson, my words would more clearly convey both the sadness I feel in the action I was compelled today to take and the firmness with which I intend to pursue this course." [31]

Finally, it should be observed that the proper exercise of the President's role requires that he speak persistently, simply, and clearly—and always with an awareness of the symbolic importance of his words and actions. The complexities of free speech, equality before the law, and due process are not grasped easily by the public. This is particularly so at a time when these constitutional values are expressed in the rhetoric of Supreme Court decisions and when the logic of extreme restraints is so convincing. Who can doubt that passports should be withheld from those with "Communist" associations? Who can doubt that "weak links" should not be employed by the government in janitorial capacities? And who can doubt that one should not be "forced" to have one's children associate with "another kind"? The Supreme Court,

[31] *New York Times*, Sept. 25, 1957. As Harry Truman explained after leaving the presidency (Harry S. Truman, *Mr. Citizen* [New York, 1960], (p. 50): "Some people do not seem to understand that it is one thing to make decisions as President and an entirely different business to make decisions as a private citizen. . . . In the White House, I never allowed myself to think that Harry Truman from Independence, Missouri, was a person deciding the fate of the world. I was deciding as President, and not as an individual thinking in terms of what he would prefer as an individual." He dramatized the point when he commented critically, as Harry Truman the Missourian, on the Southern sit-ins. See the *New York Times*, March 25, 1960.

dealing as it does with complex problems of law, is least prepared to clarify the subtle intricacies of such issues for the public at large, even though at one time President Eisenhower suggested that this was so.[32] Congress, on the other hand, tends to deal in grosser, negative symbols on the subject of liberty. A heavy responsibility then falls on the President to clarify and simplify the issues and the values at stake: one reference to Wild Bill Hickok will be worth a thousand verbal references to lawlessness.

As for the persistence of presidential efforts to inspire and instruct the nation in constitutional values it is true, as a White House aide once remarked, "If you fire the big gun too often, all you have left is a smooth bore." But, extending the metaphor, this is to misunderstand the cumulative effect of persistent small-arms fire, while reserving the big gun for moments of crisis or stress. Ideally, the President should speak persistently to bring about a broader sensitivity to the rights of others. The dramatic and adroitly timed action or communication should be reserved for specific instances to persuade the participants that their actions should be in harmony with constitutional morality. The public, as it looks on, may add this to its accumulated impressions of the values which must and will be protected.

The Instruments of Persuasion

The concrete measures available to the President to instruct and persuade the public are as various as circumstance and presidential ability permit. Almost all the instruments of persuasion assume the existence of a free press anxious to

[32] See David Riesman, "The Supreme Court and Its New Critics," *New Republic*, July 29, 1957, pp. 9–13.

carry news of the President's every word and action. Even a partial list of presidential contacts with the public and the press is impressive: his use of messages, the press conference, and the publicized findings of presidential commissions; the occasions when the President acts as ceremonial head of state or travels as the "first citizen" of the nation; and always the circumstances under which he administers and sees to the execution of the laws. All these contacts provide an opportunity for the President to help to shape public attitudes by virtue of the unique prestige of the office.

The visual image of the President, in an age of mass-circulation magazines and television, makes a White House reception more meaningful for a minority group than many days in court. In the history of presidential contact with minorities there is perhaps no more dramatic example of presidential assistance through hospitality and ceremony than Teddy Roosevelt's invitation to Booker T. Washington to visit and dine at the White House.[33] By meeting with the Negro leader, the President bestowed personal and official approval on his work and disassociated the Federal government from the cruelties of the color line, while, at the same time, he instructed his constituents to go and do likewise. The same support for those confronted by the small mind of prejudice is evidenced by President Truman's promise of Air Force transportation and an Arlington burial for the body of an American Indian who was refused interment in a Sioux City cemetery because he was not "Caucasian." These acts were symbolic expressions of the national conscience.

[33] Negro guests were invited to the major inaugural events, including the grand ball, for the first time by President Truman in 1948 (Eric F. Goldman, *The Crucial Decade* [New York, 1956], 92).

It has been frequently said that part of the President's obligation to instruct the public is to travel to points of racial disturbance in the South and elsewhere in the nation, as Presidents have done in other cases of public crisis. The symbolic effect of this type of leadership may frequently justify the cost in effort to the chief executive. Nevertheless, it should be recognized that solicitude for the time, safety, and prestige of the President will generally make it difficult for a President to appear when and where the news is being made. Some contend, for example, that a presidential appearance in Little Rock to accompany the Negro children through the line of agitators would have settled the issue or at least have brought presidential prestige to bear directly. It is just as likely that a presidential visit for this purpose would have further inflamed the opponents of desegregation and opened the President to the charge of interference with the normal processes of law enforcement. And, needless to say, the conflicting priorities of other affairs of state and the arguments of the Secret Service will severely limit such presidential activity. The President should move cautiously in such matters with an eye to the total prestige of his office and the totality of the problem at hand, with an economy of effort, and with proper staging. For the sake of mediation he should give the impression of remaining slightly removed from the battle and away from the immediacy of local ferment. This does not mean that the President's presence should be known in Washington alone. A carefully arranged visit by the President to the remains of a dynamited school or place of worship, after the event, may—with proper publicity and appropriate remarks—stamp these acts of bigotry with national disapproval while discouraging further incidents of the same sort.[34]

Although words are seldom as instructive as some dramatic step which the President might take to influence public opinion it is true nonetheless, as one authority on the presidency states, that "the words of Presidents are themselves acts, especially when spoken with conviction and persistence." [35] The pressures of a presidential day usually will force the chief executive to rely on images created for the public by means of the written or spoken word rather than action of a more direct sort. The opportunities for this type of influence on public attitudes show an interesting variety:

[34] A possible destination for a presidential visit was the Koinonia Community, an interracial Christian farm, which had been subject to assault by local segregationists for some months when the leader of the community sought the President's aid. The community was located a few miles from the President's vacation spot in Georgia. Several months of dynamiting, machine gunning, and an economic blockade had failed to produce, according to the Department of Justice, an indictable violation of Federal law. Ironically, the request to the White House for assistance was forwarded by the Department of Justice to the Governor of Georgia. Soon afterward, it is reported, the local prosecuting attorney attempted to indict the community for subversion and a variety of other crimes. As the head of the community has commented: "So all of this was the response I got from my appeal to the President of the United States" (Clarence Jordan to the author, March 14, 1959). Although an actual trip to the beleaguered community may have been precluded by the President's understandable need for rest and recuperation, the gravity of the threat to the group and the strange inadequacy of the state police power perhaps called for some sort of statement by the President. See the *Christian Century*, March 6, 1957, and Eugene J. Lipman, "Report on a Siege," *ibid.*, Feb. 25, 1959.

[35] Louis W. Koenig, *The Truman Administration* (New York, 1956), 94.

affirmative statements in the State of the Union Message and other special messages to Congress and to private groups; private conferences with opinion leaders in the South and other parts of the nation; the careful selection of comments in the President's press conferences; the extending of presidential greetings to private groups working in the field of civil liberties and minority rights; and public or confidential communications with individuals who are seeking support for the preservation of constitutional guarantees.

All Presidents receive numberless requests from private groups for presidential greetings endorsing their existence and activities.[36] By appearing before libertarian groups or sending a message the President can support their principles and extend the sphere of his own educational effectiveness. Presidential correspondence, in turn, may be directed to public consumption or as private pleas to the recipients for aid to the President in his own efforts to influence certain public groups. He may attack public attitudes by open correspondence, as President Truman did when he replied to a complaint that a member of his administration was a supporter of the World Federalists:

"All this howl about organizations a fellow belongs to," the President declared, "gives me a pain in the neck. I'd be willing to bet my right eye that you yourself and I have joined some organizations that we wish we hadn't. It hasn't hurt me any and I don't think it has hurt you any." [37]

[36] For instance, almost the entire contents of File 4762 in the Franklin D. Roosevelt Papers, Roosevelt Library, Hyde Park, N.Y. deals with requests for presidential appearances.

[37] President Truman to the Commander of the Veterans of Foreign Wars (Clyde A. Lewis), New York Times, June 7, 1950.

The letter, which was publicized soon after Senator Mc-Carthy discovered communism, was a partial presidential reply to the prevailing public commitment to guilt by association, a reply which the President sustained also in public speeches, most notably his address to the American Legion on "true Americanism." Similarly, one of President Eisenhower's strongest statements in support of equal rights, as well as a declaration of his own responsibility, appears in his State of the Union Message delivered in January, 1959. "Those of us who are privileged to hold public office," the President said, "have a solemn obligation to make [the equal protection of the laws] meaningful. We can fulfill that obligation by our leadership in *teaching, persuading, demonstrating, and enforcing the law.*" [38]

Of all means for "teaching and persuading" the public, few are as fruitful—or as potentially damaging—as the presidential press conference. Not only will the President receive from the press news of shortcomings within his administration, but the direct simplicity of his replies will return to the nation with a speed, if not always with a clarity, denied to most other forms of presidential communication. The press conference enables the President to alert his administration and Congress, to express his favor for one interest or value over another, and to dramatize the intensity of his feelings. The public will note presidential equivocation or determination, as it did President Eisenhower's resolve, in the fall of 1958, not to countenance open defiance of court decrees. As mentioned earlier, President

[38] State of the Union Message, *New York Times*, Jan. 10, 1959. Emphasis added.

Eisenhower failed to give unequivocal support to the traditional protection against self-incrimination. It led a commentator, not known for his radicalism, to remark:

> It would have been a service to one of the greatest barriers ever erected by free men against tyranny if the President had added this acknowledgement of the purpose of the Fifth Amendment. It stands in need of defenders because of the motives for which it has been invoked on many occasions in recent times.[39]

Because the press conference may produce the unexpected question, the President's personal attitudes are likely to be exposed, as they were when President Truman referred unguardedly to a congressional investigation of communism as a "red herring." As a consequence, a President must strive to speak in measured and responsible terms. At the same time, the effectiveness of his words is increased by a distinctive and news-worthy spontaneity which is seldom found among the complexities and carefully planned phrases of a formal address.

Other Instruments of Persuasion

The occasional remarks of the President must be supplemented by a more systematic pattern of persuasion if his efforts to influence the various publics are to attain any real degree of effectiveness. There are administrative means which enable the President to bring together publicity, consultation, and *expertise* to inform the nation. The President's Committee on Government Contracts and conferences called by the Committee have already been alluded to. Other

[39] Arthur Krock in the *New York Times*, March 28, 1957.

presidential committees in recent years (some strengthened by congressional authorization) include the President's Commission on Higher Education (1948), which condemned discrimination in colleges and universities, the President's Committee on Civil Rights, and the Civil Rights Commission authorized by the Civil Rights Act of 1957.

The most successful organization of this type was the Truman Committee on Civil Rights, established by the President in a period of incipient crisis in race relations. Responding to the request of a Negro delegation, and particularly angered by the blackjack blinding of a Negro veteran at the hands of a South Carolina police chief, the President created the Committee by executive order in 1946.[40] He avoided unnecessary delay and legislative barriers by paying the Committee's expenses from the President's contingency fund. As he declared later: "As President of the United States I felt I ought to do everything within my power to find what caused such crimes and root out the causes." [41]

No concrete legislation issued directly from the Committee's report, *To Secure These Rights*, although it seems to have affected the climate favorably in the courts and Congress. The most important immediate effect was to inform the public—and the President—of the shortcomings of the nation in civil rights. Its statement of principles pro-

[40] The Department of Justice was interested in the Committee as a means for re-evaluating the existing civil rights statutes and proposing reform. See Walter White, *A Man Called White* (New York, 1948), 331, and *How Far the Promised Land* (New York, 1956), 76; Truman, *Memoirs: Years of Trial and Hope* (New York, 1956), 180.

[41] Koenig, *The Truman Administration*, 118.

vided a yardstick for public policy, and the details of the report became an important source of information. This combination of official fact and opinion by a presidentially designated body remains a challenging illustration of the usefulness of this medium of persuasion. The significance of active presidential support for commissions of this kind is illustrated amply by the hospitality and enthusiasm with which President Truman received the report of his presidentially appointed commission and President Eisenhower's aloofness when the Commission on Civil Rights, appointed after considerable delay by the President but established by Congress, reported to the nation in 1959. The first commission was established and supported actively by President Truman, the second commission was a congressional stepchild which never seemed to stir the interest of his successor. Although the accomplishments of the latter commission were impressive—particularly the studies which were made of voting restrictions in the South and discrimination in housing—its effectiveness was reduced by virtue of presidential distance.

Government by consent presupposes the free acceptance of the values of a constitutional society, and, ideally, persuasion is an educative act. The role of a presidential commission is to attempt to inform and to produce consent. Nonetheless, persuasion must sometimes take direct advantage of pure self-interest, where consent, in effect, is bartered for. Such consent is fickle, but, for those who feel no compunction against interfering with the rights of others, the bestowal or denial of rewards by the Federal executive may be the only attractive medium of exchange. The proposition can be stated in different terms. Why, the Federal government may ask, should funds, insofar as the executive controls their distribution, move unchecked into a state which denies to some of its citizens the equal protection of the laws? Why, further, should Federal contracts be given to firms which discriminate unfairly in their hiring policies? And why should the perquisites of office, including patronage, be given to politicians whose political ambitions are nurtured by demagogy or turbulence? As one administrator experienced in this field has remarked:

The Federal government of today . . . is a dynamic sovereignty whose influence reaches into every aspect of the economy and its people. Its welfare power is now substantive, its other powers extensive; it is the greatest single source for spending and lending for new ventures; it finances housing and city development, controls credit, insures investments, grants huge subsidies to private and public agencies; it builds dams, atom plants, roads and public works. Its influence permeates almost every phase of enterprise and touches every local official and citizen.

He concludes: "Resistance to the law [and, one might add, attacks on liberty of any kind] has always proven costly and should never be made cheap." [42] There is, in other words, enough in the way of presidential patronage and Federal money to help to buy consent. In many cases credit may be withheld, or subsidies distributed, in such a way as to express executive dissatisfaction with discriminative policies. A President can discourage Federal expenditures where they may be tainted by the violation of constitutional guarantees. In many instances, but hardly all, political and community leaders will be willing to trade the political and economic

[42] Abrams, "New York and Little Rock."

profits of discrimination for Federal assistance and co-operation. Further, those who were indifferent to denials of equal protection may be convinced that it is not officially condoned and that it does not pay.

In many respects this is one of the most promising of all the frontiers for executive action in the service of civil rights. By executive order and executive direction Federal public housing expenditures or the mortgage guarantees under FHA programs may be administered in a way that will discourage discrimination and continued segregation; Federal grants for the construction of airports and other facilities in the states may prohibit the encumbrances of segregated facilities or discrimination in their use; and Federal contracts may be withheld until the requirements of nondiscriminatory hiring and promotion are met. The deep social patterns and personal conveniences associated with segregation and discrimination may be shaken by White House pressure and by threatened restrictions on Federal largess where those who would accept Federal funds will not accept a concomitant responsibility to constitutional rights. Clearly this instrument of "persuasion" must be used with the utmost caution. The President's determinination to extinguish discrimination by executive order in programs dependent on Federal money should, however, be stated emphatically and, as an ultimate goal, diligently pursued. Yet it must be recognized that popular consent is not a commodity in the market place; some persons, particularly those in political life, will be reached by this kind of bargain, but in others it may create destructive resentment rather than co-operation. Further, the denial of funds or other Federal emoluments may damage a program in which there is an overriding national interest despite the existence of discrimination. In such cases, as in Federal aid to education, the problem may have to be attacked in other ways. In sum, the presumption should run strongly against an automatic grant of Federal money to communities or programs which will taint that money. On the other hand, this instrument of persuasion should be used as a lever, not a sledge hammer; it must be applied with determination, but also with restraint.

Finally, just as prudent administration of Federal monies and perquisites may educate and persuade, so may the President when he sees to the faithful execution of the law. Whether the law is of statutory or judicial origin, the vigor and sense with which it is executed will have a definite impact on the public image of what is morally and constitutionally correct. Law is itself an ingredient of public education; and proper enforcement of the letter of the law will build customary obedience and assist in consummating consent. If the lessons of the law are to be learned and the law itself is to be respected, much will depend on the quality and diligence of enforcement, a responsibility in Federal law which falls squarely on the President.

When Louis Brandeis joined with Justice Holmes in condemning wire tapping as "dirty business," he stated: "Our government is the potent, omnipresent teacher. For good or ill, it teaches the whole people by its example." [43] Quality in law enforcement, where individual liberties are directly involved, lies in correct procedure which will ultimately combine respect for the law with respect for the law enforcer. If the operations of the FBI show restraint, if the proceed-

[43] Dissenting opinion in *Olmstead* v. *United States,* 277 U.S. 438, 485 (1928).

211

ings before security boards follow due process of law, or if vindictiveness and partisanship are absent from Department of Justice prosecutions, the best constitutional values will be reflected in the act of enforcement. The quality of enforcement will tend to spread the image of what is constitutionally correct to individual citizens and law enforcement agencies throughout the Federal structure.

As for diligence in law enforcement, public knowledge that the law will really be enforced to protect minority rights, for example, will help to dissuade the violator and, among the hostile and indifferent, transform the law into a symbol of a determined national conscience. Diligence, not timidity, should govern the executive in the protection of voting rights or in the enforcement of court orders calling for desegregation. Law in action provides an instrumental definition and clarification of constitutional principles. It counteracts the twisted energy of those who would defy constituted authority and enables those who wish to obey to attach themselves to a "respect for the law." Even thoughtful citizens "need and want their consciences bolstered by law," [44] and they seek a system which expresses a high constitutional standard.

As for the adage that law or law enforcement cannot create folkways, it is true only if one assumes that there is no difference between prejudice and discrimination or that there are no parallel means of persuasion. Prejudices are beliefs which call for distance from other persons; discrimination is an act which seeks to impose this distance arti-

[44] Gordon W. Allport, *The Nature of Prejudice* (New York, 1958), 439. See Charles Black, Jr., "Paths to Desegregation," *New Republic*, Oct. 21, 1957, pp. 10–15.

fically. The law need not countenance constitutionally irrelevant discrimination, that is, public classification of persons on the basis of race; and though prejudice cannot be stifled directly by law, law can establish a new framework which itself may "inhibit the acting out of prejudices and provide the opportunities for prejudiced persons to have experiences which may change their minds and hearts." [45] Furthermore, law may provide the situation in which other forces, including presidential leadership, may operate to ameliorate popular mores. The faithful execution of laws which attack racial discrimination can discourage the stagnation of old ways. As Justice Frankfurter wrote in his brilliant concurring opinion in *Cooper* v. *Aaron:*

Local customs, however hardened by time, are not decreed in heaven. Habits and feelings they engender may be counteracted and moderated. Experience attests that such local habits and feelings will yield, gradually though this be, to law and education. And educational influences are exerted not only by explicit teaching. They vigorously flow from the fruitful exercise of the responsibility of those charged with political official power and from the almost unconsciously transforming actualities of living under the law.[46]

In the field of minority rights, the executive is especially endowed to uphold the equation, now constitutionally applicable for desegregation, that what is lawful is right and what is lawful will be enforced. When the dust settles, an

[45] George M. Johnson, "The United States Commission on Civil Rights" (Address to the 1959 Annual Convention of the Federal Bar Association in Washington, D.C., Sept. 25, 1959 [mimeo.]); Melvin Tumin, *Desegregation, Resistance, and Readiness* (New York, 1959).

[46] 358 U.S. 1, 25 (1958).

event like Little Rock will be remembered for its educational effect, although this imperfect operation will have clarified a further lesson in executive persuasion: that other educational efforts must precede the use of force and that tactless application may harden the uneducated.

Public Opinion and School Desegregation

The months which span the period between the Supreme Court's decision on segregation in the public schools and the violence in Little Rock contain the story of a lost presidential opportunity. At a time when most of the instruments of presidential persuasion and guidance should have been put to use, the White House was virtually inactive. In the light of the President's obligation to attempt to instruct the American public, presidential quiescence after the Supreme Court's decision in 1954 provides a telling example of what a President might have done and did not. As opposition to the Supreme Court decision grew in the South, long presidential silences were broken only by half-developed statements of constitutional and social propriety expressed in a spirit of puzzled good will. Southern statements of defiance of the Supreme Court and other signs of resistance to the law met with no national counterforce.

When the Supreme Court first handed down its decision, there was a general air of sullen and, in many cases, relieved acceptance in the South. Then the President might have used instruments of leadership at his disposal. Even later, as the tide turned against acceptance, presidential power might have been a remedy for recalcitrance. Instead the only official voices were the Federal courts, the Southern legislatures, and the manifesto of defiance signed by the Southern

214

delegation in Congress. "What the hell do you expect these people to do when they have 90 some odd Congressmen from the South signing a piece of paper that says you're a southern hero if you defy the Supreme Court," one Clinton, Tennessee, lawyer remarked after violence erupted over desegregation there.[47]

When the President might have attempted to counteract the flood of misinformation coming from the South by calling conferences of school administrators, law enforcement officers, and others or have spoken officially through a presidential commission and with his own voice, these powers lay largely unused. He did not speak persistently of the rich harvest for Communist propaganda inherent in segregation nor did he give guidance and support to groups directly engaged in this social crisis. There is no evidence that the President encouraged opinion leaders in the South —owners of newspapers and television stations, ministers, industrialists, and others often associated with incipient moderation—to help influence the public mood. And before the dispatch of troops to Little Rock there was no major presidential address on desegregation. In a word, the White House was not used as a center of national leadership on the issue.

Whatever the reasons for this policy of disengagement, it seems to have been rooted in a basic misconception: that the President should and could avoid personal or official involvement in this critical period of social change. It is reflected not only in the over-all posture of disengagement but most markedly in the President's refusal to express him-

[47] Don Shoemaker, *With All Deliberate Speed* (New York, 1957), 38.

self on the "morality" of the Supreme Court's decision. When the problem of enforcement arose, then, indeed, the President came quickly to a consistent decision that the decrees of the Federal judiciary must be executed, but until then he seemed inhibited by what he described as the difficulty in changing the "hearts of men." By failing to commit the White House to a position opposed to the primitive "moral" arguments of the most extreme segregationists he sheathed one of his most effective weapons—a long-term appeal to the conscience of the South. As one study of racial trouble in Tennessee concluded: "There is need for someone . . . to say 'Desegregation is right,' as well as, 'It is the law.'"[48] Segregationists there dealt with desegregation as a moral and social issue and banked on the inclination of citizens to avoid obeying law which was not "right." Here, as elsewhere, the absence of a series of ringing presidential pronouncements defending the constitutional propriety of desegregation aided those who defied the law. This theory of inaction is of such importance that it should be described in the President's own words:

I have always declined [to state my personal opinion on desegregation] for the simple reason that here was something that the Supreme Court says this is the direction of the Constitution, this is the instruction of the Constitution. That is, they say this is the meaning of the Constitution.

Now, I am sworn to one thing, to defend the Constitution of the United States and execute its laws. Therefore, for me to weaken public opinion by discussion of complete—separate

---

[48] Preston Valien *et al.*, *Clinton, Tennessee: A Tentative Description and Analysis of the School Desegregation Crisis* (Anti-Defamation League of B'nai B'rith, New York, n.d.), 23.

cases, where I might agree or disagree, seems to me to be completely unwise and not a good thing to do.

I have an oath; I expect to carry it out. And the mere fact that I could disagree very violently with a decision, and would so express myself, then my own duty would be much more difficult to carry out I think. So I think it is just not good business for me to do so.[49]

This exposes significant flaws in the President's reasoning. His personal opinion was not at issue; what was at issue was his official opinion on the desirability of attacking the constitutional absurdity of unequal protection of the laws. Second, this was not just another Supreme Court decision but one which touched the vital core of professed national beliefs about equality before the law. And third, in respect to the President's obligation to public opinion, the lesson of the President's logic is contrary to the premise. Official presidential agreement with the principle of desegregation would not have weakened public opinion but, to the contrary, would have strengthened those who wished to uphold the law, thus re-enforcing the President's power to see to the execution of the laws. As Walter Lippmann remarked of the President's comment:

The integration of the public schools of the Deep South poses the most difficult internal problem which has appeared in this century, and the President's conception of his role in dealing with the problem is so abstract, so generalized, and so unrealistic that he will not even say whether he believes in the principle which he has used Federal troops to enforce.[50]

[49] The President's press conference, *New York Times*, Aug. 21, 1958.

[50] "Law without Policy," *Washington Post and Times Herald*, Aug. 26, 1958.

The President's reluctance to take the lead in persuading the public and generating consent did not just reduce the number of voices by one. It removed the presidency from this elemental part of the democratic process at a time when national leadership was needed. Silence and apparent confusion about the constitutional obligation of the chief executive played into the hands of the segregationists who were, apparently, by no means confused. In brief, the President based his case for inaction on the need for strong public opinion and an eventual change in the hearts of men and yet was not actively engaged in bringing the change about.[51] The same general attitude of disengagement manifested itself in the President's reaction to the lunch counter "sit-in" demonstrations in 1960. At the height of this peaceful effort, the President remarked that these matters had come to his attention only "briefly" and that although he believed some of the demonstrations were "a proper expression of a conviction of the group making them" he refused to make any over-all judgment because he, the President, was "not in a position to." [52]

[51] For eloquent statements of the need for education in the nation on desegregation see the President's press conferences in the *New York Times*, Sept. 6, 1956, and March 27, 1958.

[52] The President's press conference, *New York Times*, March 17, 1960. See the remarks of James Reston, *ibid.*, March 18, 1960: "There are a lot of people here who. . . . think the President, one hundred years after Appomattox, ought to be willing to say at least a word for the Negro trying to eat a hamburger next to a white man in Atlanta." The Attorney General, William P. Rogers, who though sometimes cautious possessed a sound record on civil rights matters, improved the President's position by inaugurating partially successful conferences with the executives of national chain stores to bring about some desegregation at their lunch counters in the South.

Finally, a word should be said about the President's further forswearing of an active role when the Supreme Court was under attack. Those who mounted the assault on the Court in mid-1955 (an attack which culminated in the surprisingly lively Jenner-Butler bill to restrict the jurisdiction of the Supreme Court) were aided by the lack of presidential endorsement of the desegregation decision and, more directly, by presidential reticence throughout the period of assault. Although perhaps advisable, it was not necessary for the President to defend the specific decisions which were criticized in Congress; rather, it was his firm constitutional obligation to defend the function and independence of the Supreme Court. The Department of Justice opposed the Jenner-Butler bill in Congress, but the statements of the President at a time when the public needed reassurance and sound information were inadequate.

A new awareness and a shift in the administration's outlook after the "first Little Rock war" indicated that the White House and the Department of Justice were beginning to comprehend a double truth: that without the support of the executive branch the Court was powerless to protect itself against public and congressional opinion and that the resurgence of resistance to desegregation in the South called for more than a formal affirmation of the legality of the Supreme Court's original desegregation finding. The President reiterated his intention to enforce court decrees with troops if necessary although he refused again in the same breath to support the wisdom of the decision. This lapse was repaired somewhat in a well-publicized letter to a Virginia correspondent in which the President spoke of desegregation as "being contrary to one of the generally accepted basic ideals of our country . . . that all men are equal in the sight of God" and in a press conference statement in 1959 that interference with equality of opportunity in the economic and political fields was morally wrong. In addition, the Attorney General's office began a cautious campaign to educate the country and re-educate the nation's lawyers on the importance of judicial independence.[53] There seemed to be an awakening to presidential obligation, after three years of uncertainty.

Conclusion

As Woodrow Wilson wrote in 1908:

[The President is the] spokesman for the real sentiment and purpose of the country, by giving direction to opinion, by giving the country at once the information and the statements of policy which will enable it to form its own judgments alike of parties and of men. . . .

His is the only national voice in affairs. Let him once win the admiration and confidence of the country, and no other single force can withstand him, no combination of forces will easily overpower him. His position takes the imagination of the country. He is representative of no constituency, but of the whole people.[54]

[53] *New York Times*, July 9, 1959. The President's letter to J. Albert Rolston appears in the *Washington Post and Times Herald*, Sept. 26, 1958. See, for example, the Attorney General's speech to the National Conference on Citizenship, *New York Times*, Sept. 18, 1958, and the account of Solicitor General Rankin's speech in *ibid.*, March 14, 1959.

[54] *Constitutional Government in the United States* (New York, 1908), 68.

There was no reason to suppose in 1908 that the responsibility to lead public opinion would broaden and intensify to become an obligation to constitutional guarantees in a period of perpetual Cold War and critical social change in civil rights. The powers a President derives from public support are the same, but a new dimension has been added. The President today must sometimes give the country information which his own bureaucracy would withhold on grounds of national security. He can utilize, as well, the instruments of persuasion and instruction which are uniquely presidential to create concrete and positive images of citizen responsibility toward the rights of others. He may guide the opinions of both the general public and particular publics in the present period of sharp change in civil rights, and he can oppose a national tendency to subordinate constitutional guarantees to ritual loyalty and security. He is empowered, in sum, to defend for and against the public the constitutional processes on which the character of the nation rests.

That the role is difficult, that there may be little likelihood of consistent success, does not change the President's obligation to remind the public of constitutional values or to sense the consequences of his own indifference.

VI

Action, Counteraction,
and Accommodation

AT one time in 1958 American troops were keeping the peace in such widely separated points of crisis as Lebanon and Little Rock. Each contingent was dispatched by the President's order, a fact which in itself suggests the ultimate unity of the chief executive's obligation to defend both the nation and its system of constitutional rights. In each year of the Cold War period some event—whether involving the bayonets in Little Rock, the desegregated mingling of Negroes and whites among the troops in Lebanon, the pitiful confusion among the departments over the loyalty-security program, or the executive hectoring over passports —testified to the depth of administrative immersion in the inseparable problems of liberty and security. Presidential power today is dedicated primarily to the maintenance of national security, a fact which both creates and intensifies a correlative obligation to constitutional rights. Although the two frequently seem to clash, the clash itself must not deflect men from the search for a working harmony between them or conceal the stark fact of the futility of liberty without security or of security without liberty. The array of instruments which enable the President to protect constitutional guarantees is an imposing one; the difficulties in using them effectively are immeasurable. The instruments, of course, may be mishandled or may be wielded to undermine constitutional liberty. But once used with vision and determination, the means available are capable of preserving traditional guarantees and adjusting them to the necessities of the Cold War and social change.

As has been demonstrated in the preceding pages, although the President cannot move blindly against the grain of national sentiment or the power of Congress and the judiciary, his power can, nevertheless, be effective in shaping legislation or inhibiting congressional immoderation. He has, moreover, the authority to encourage a new direction within the administration by questioning and shaking up deeply entrenched administrative attitudes while, as chief executive, he can encourage law enforcement which is responsive to justice as well as efficiency. In his official pronouncements, furthermore, the public will hear, if not always accept, his words of guidance and warning: both as major-domo of his administration and as popular leader, the President can exert his influence as symbol and guardian of the best constitutional sense of the nation.

Needless to say, an exertion of power in a constitutional system is never unilinear; the affirmative use of power does not lead inexorably to a predictable result. Rather, the President's use of power to protect individual liberties, as in other instances, takes place in the complicating presence of his other obligations and of countervailing institutions. The President will always struggle against an exhausting paucity of time and a profusion of tangled priorities. The simple equation of action and result must give way, then, to a closer approximation of institutional reality, best described as a process of action, counteraction, and accommodation. Rare are the occasions when the President has sufficient control over circumstances, both political and institutional, to propose and carry through a program of his own design. What is proposed will tend to change shape, to lose and add substance, in each stage of the process of its coming into being. The President must act in order to forestall other political forces; but always his action must be keyed to a recognition that the result will probably be only an approximation of his original wishes. More often than not he will find himself dealing with half-apparent realities which can be handled only by counteraction. He may be able to bend political actuality to a new direction or stifle its energy; seldom will he be able to reverse its course. While the realities of presidential leadership minimize action and maximize counteraction, the President's political and institutional responsibilities require him also to accommodate competing interests and values. This does not mean that he must give way to shapeless opportunism, for the supreme dictates of the national interest and the Constitution establish the limits. But still he must attempt to take into account the demands and sentiments of various groups within the community; none can be crushed or ignored. The President is not able and should not be able to impose a unilateral solution—except when the highest needs of national security require it —without regard to its effect on all segments of the political community.

This pattern of action, counteraction, and accommodation

suggests one way of capturing the essence of presidential leadership both generally and in the field of individual liberties in particular. In one degree or another all three elements will be present as the executive attempts to lead, although all must be geared ultimately to the salutary inflexibility of constitutional standards and national survival. The institutional problem is to discover, at a given moment, the optimum assertion of each which presidential capability, circumstance, and constitutional limitations will permit. When presidential leadership is viewed in this light, its complexity, richness, possibilities, and difficulties become more understandable.

Almost every problem that a President meets in the field of constitutional rights is illuminated by this scheme. For example, it is one of the major themes of this study that presidential action between 1954 and the 1957 eruption in Little Rock was strikingly deficient. There was much that the President could have done to help to prepare the South for this crisis in race relations. These measures, nonetheless, could not possibly have guaranteed the total absence of local disturbance in Little Rock or elsewhere. When political forces were set in motion and combined with a peculiar set of accidents and intentions, the President could do no more than react to circumstances forced upon him. Federal intervention rested on a series of "ifs" momentarily beyond presidential control. As Brooks Hays has written:

There were speculations as to what might have happened "if": If the Governor had not gone away, and if he had sent state police to patrol actively the school area (he had never said he would not); If it had not been a bright clear day (it had rained hard the two previous days); If the fire chief had responded to Mayor Mann's request for the use of the fire hose; If Judge Davies had ordered the United States marshal to assist the local police and add to his force of deputies; If there had been a permanent federal judge presiding who had been appointed from the district; and, If the situation had arisen after, instead of before, the new city-manager form of government had been installed.

Thus it was that a combination of factors conspired against the success of the move to integrate peacefully the nine Negro students.[1]

In this way, the problem was forced onto the President's desk, one problem among many others, and positive steps were taken in a larger framework of counteraction. Throughout the crisis, furthermore, he was institutionally and politically bound to search for accommodation among competing methods and interests. In 1958 accommodation, however excessive it may ultimately be judged, was the rule. In Virginia the Department of Justice limited its action to *amicus curiae* appearances while the administration urged compliance with court decrees. The President made clear that the integrity of the judicial process would be upheld by the executive. The tactic of accommodation, however wise, was apparent, too, in the acceptance by Attorney General Rogers of fairly administered pupil placement laws as a working Southern solution for desegregation and in the reluctance of the administration in 1960 to press for legislation empowering the Department of Justice to originate desegregation cases in the Federal courts.[2]

[1] Brooks Hays, *A Southern Moderate Speaks* (Chapel Hill, 1959), 173–174.

[2] *Washington Post and Times Herald,* Jan. 24, 1959.

The same configuration is evident in other presidential attacks on discrimination and in the operation of the security programs. When the administration deals with discrimination on the part of firms under contract to the government, an outright, punitive program may do more harm than good. The executive moves to counteract prejudice but has tended to rely in the past on accommodation and conciliation; to move too swiftly may jeopardize competing governmental interests (such as urgent defense production) or the program itself. Only a delicate balance of initiative and negotiation, will, according to official government philosophy, bring the elimination of this type of discrimination.

As for the security programs—whether affecting government personnel, passports, or government information policies—the same pattern prevails. In the loyalty-security program the White House has taken some affirmative action in proposing reforms, and it must, moreover, be remembered that presidential action established the programs in the first place. But the predominant cast of policy has been one of counteraction: to Congress, to the pleas of security officers, and—when presidential influence has been used beneficially —to combat mistakes spawned by the system itself. Throughout, Presidents have attempted to accommodate the competing claims of constitutional guarantees, political necessity, and security.

What is true of each problem as it arises is no less true of each of the presidential functions as they been presented in this study. The White House may be disinclined to propose, or unable to carry through, affirmative *legislative* proposals; often, rather, the chief executive will have to respond to what Congress proposes, or is about to propose, while attempting to bring about some agreement among the various political and administrative interests, chief among them the security agencies. If he looks to his primary responsibility for national security, he cannot afford to affront certain groups in Congress by presenting an uncompromising and time-consuming legislative program in the civil rights field, while in all direct legislative proposals the executive must blend the legitimate interests of the police agencies with an allowance for restraint on their power. In the *administrative* sphere he is in a better position to take affirmative action in the expectation of unimpeded success. Nonetheless, because the bureaucracy in many respects is not responsive to presidential direction and because of the barriers of size and conflicting interests within an administration, even in administrative policy the President will find himself serving as accommodator of competing values and personalities or counterpoised against practices originating deep within the executive branch. In the *execution* of the laws, presidential initiative is perhaps most untrammeled, for affirmative action will, more often than not, lead to a predicted result. On the other hand, the chief executive must counteract unimaginative rigidity in executing the law and must guard against the zeal of prosecuting and investigatory agencies. Sound enforcement policies may require, furthermore, executive adjustment to local conditions and self-restraint in enforcement where the letter of the law might be upheld but the individual unjustly punished. Finally, in exercising his responsibility to *public opinion* the President can be effectively active in shaping national attitudes toward individual freedom. Frequently this will take the form of counteracting sentiment which wells up from the public itself or emanates from other centers of political power. But even here accommodation is required: he must face the delicate responsibility of alerting the nation to threats to the national security while defending constitutional guarantees against public and political attack. In dealing with national attitudes toward civil rights an open mind must accompany reasoned firmness; if the President is to build consent in this field, empty moralizing or Federal self-righteousness may do more harm than good.

The American presidency need not be paralyzed by this multidimensional view of presidential leadership. There are guiding principles, which, if firmly held and vigorously applied, provide the White House with momentum and direction. For the President, these principles embrace a consciousness of the traditions of the office and a willingness to use his powers. The vitality of presidential power, furthermore, originates in the incumbent's acceptance of his role as the one national leader in matters of national security and economic welfare. In regard to the President's specific obligation to protect individual liberties, the guiding principles are found among the traditional constitutional guarantees and the adherence to law itself.

The principles are well settled if not always easy to apply. Essentially they require decency and fairness when the government deals with the individual, values which are embedded in the concept of due process of law; they assume further a consciousness of the individual's right to develop creatively through free inquiry, unhampered by unnecessary governmental restrictions. The responsibility of the White House is stimulated only when the President is sensitive to his own important role in defending the bedrock of constitutional rights or has an acute sense of the consequences of executive indifference. For lack of this, momentum will fade and true direction will be lost; policy will follow the interest of the currently powerful political and public forces or the raw needs of the security agencies. Furthermore, if the White House is to avoid mere drift or the fits and starts of intermittent decisions in this field, it would be well for a President to settle on certain maxims and attach his power to them. These may be stated in a variety of ways, but the following seem to grow out of the present study:

1. The White House has a vital role to play as a moderating force against the ubiquitous police and military mentality of the Cold War period. Security-mindedness should confront the need for a pervasive acceptance of "risk," if a free society is to thrive. The presidential office should maintain a close guard over all security programs and a persistent if not stubborn presumption against the validity of measures which might affect constitutional guarantees.

2. The White House should accept as a constitutional necessity the participation of the Federal executive in efforts to improve the nation's record in civil rights. Whatever executive instrument may be used in a given situation, the administrative presumption should be unremitting opposition to discrimination and denials of the equal protection of the law.

3. The President should be provided with open channels of information, both official and unofficial, in order to increase his awareness and knowledge of programmatic and individual violations of constitutional rights. Provision should

be made for regular and systematic consideration of this information.

4. The qualifications for appointment to certain key positions in the executive branch should include an estimate of the value which an appointee attaches to constitutional restraints.

5. A President should be aware that his words and acts help to build an image of official attitudes toward individual liberties. He should avoid confusing his personal opinion with his constitutional opinion. In the public mind they tend to merge into a single view of what the government represents, not what the incumbent believes.

These precepts will seldom dominate policy making. To expect Presidents and their advisers to seek and find a conclusive equilibrium between liberty and security or to presume that the presidential office can move majestically above the battle of politics and administrative self-interest would be to delude further those who expect too much of the President. The crushing burden on the President as well as the limitations which "politics" and federalism impose on his power can never be overlooked. What is possible, however, once the critical nature of presidential responsibility is recognized, is the unremitting application of these precepts and a close adherence to constitutional standards in policy formulation. The equilibrium should always be sought: the impulse to rise above the temptation of immediate political gain and administrative convenience should always be present. The bothersome question of how policy will affect individual liberty must be repeatedly introduced, unless the executive mainstay of our constitutional

231

rights is to erode. Once these factors are understood, much can be done; but much will always remain to be done.

Traditionally, executive power has been viewed as antagonistic to individual liberty. Although there is abundant evidence in recent years of the misuse of executive power, the essential genius of the American presidency has made it a liberating rather than constricting force in the American scheme of constitutionalism. It is this quality which must be reaffirmed by the White House whenever the executive power and constitutional guarantees threaten to clash. The dangers inherent in the executive power should call forth self-restraint within the executive branch and an elementary reign of vigilance by Congress and the judiciary. But the President's responsibility goes beyond self-restraint alone. In harmony with the traditions of the office and a compelling constitutional obligation, it calls for the positive intervention of the White House to protect and invigorate the liberating substance of the Constitution.

Index